KIERAN BEVILLE

Cultivating Christian Character

The Fruit of the Spirit

DayOne

© Day One Publications 2005
First printed 2005

ISBN 1 903087 78-3

9 781903 087787

Unless otherwise stated, all Scripture quotations are from the
New International Version copyright © 2002

British Library Cataloguing in Publication Data available

Published by Day One Publications
Ryelands Road, Leominster, HR6 8NZ
☎ 01568 613 740 FAX 01568 611 473
email—sales@dayone.co.uk
web site—www.dayone.co.uk
North American—e-mail—sales@dayonebookstore.com
North American—web site—www.dayonebookstore.com

Designed by Steve Devane and printed by Gutenberg Press, Malta

For:
Ferdia, Eoin and Aoife.
'I have no greater joy than to hear that my
children are walking in the truth'
(3 John 4).

Contents

Acknowledgements

I have cited a small number of sources in the footnotes where reference is made to authors and their works, giving details of publishers/dates and page numbers. I have also quoted other works without detailed annotation. In all such instances I have attributed the words to the relevant author. The reason for omitting footnotes in some cases is simply to avoid repetitiously mentioning two books that I used to glean quotations. I wish, therefore, to acknowledge that, *More Gathered Gold: a treasury of quotations for Christians*, compiled by John Blanchard and published by Evangelical Press in 1986, has helped to add grandeur to this work. The Calvin quotations are taken from *Calvin's Wisdom: An Anthology Arranged Alphabetically* by J. Graham Miller; published in 1992 by The Banner of Truth Trust. I hope this has not inadvertently conveyed the impression that my book is a work of scholarly research. Rather this work began its life as a series of sermons on *The Fruit of the Spirit* which have been further developed for publication.

An abridged version of the 'Introduction' was serialised in three parts under the title 'Cultivating Christian Character' (*Evangelical Times:* July, August and September, 2004). Some of the chapter on 'Kindness' first appeared as an article entitled, *'A Place At The Top Table'* (*Evangelical Times*, August 2002). The chapter on 'Gentleness' contains my article, 'The 'Diploma Disease' (*Evangelical Times*, August 2003). I am grateful to the editors, Roger Fay and Edgar Andrews for featuring these and more of my articles over the last few years. A shortened version of the chapter on 'Love', featured as 'Learning in Love' (*The Banner of Truth*, November 2004). I am very thankful to the editor, Walter Chantry, for publishing this and other articles of mine. This first chapter also contains a modified version of my article 'The Compassionate Character of Christ' (*The Gospel Magazine*, July-August 2003). I wish to express my appreciation to the editor, Rev. Edward Malcolm, for publishing some of my work. The chapter on 'Joy' contains my article 'A Mosaic of the Master' (*The Monthly Record*, April 2003). Thanks to the editor, Alex MacDonald, for publishing it. Some of this chapter also appeared as 'The Place of Humour in Preaching' (*Preaching: The Professional Journal for Preachers*, USA, January-February 2004 and also in *Evangelicals Now*, November 2003). I am grateful to the respective editors, Michael Duduit, for publishing my

Acknowledgements

unabridged version and to John Benton for featuring this and other articles of mine. Part of the chapter on 'Goodness' appeared as: 'Unconditional Election: Based on Objections to Foreknowledge' (*Grace Magazine*, October 2004). I am thankful to the editor, Tim Curnow, for publishing it.

I am greatly indebted to the congregation of Westside Baptist Church (who first heard these chapters in sermon form) for generously allowing me some personal leave. This book is the fruit of that time out.

I would also like to thank my dear friends Eddie Dorney and Terry Price for their tremendous encouragement at a time when it was most needed.

I hope the reader will find insight and inspiration in these pages.

Kieran Beville

'But the fruit of the Spirit is love, joy, peace, patience, kindness, goodness, faithfulness, gentleness and self-control ...' (Galatians 5:22–23).

Here in chapter five of Paul's letter to the Galatian church we have a beautiful portrait of the fruit of the Holy Spirit. It is a cluster of nine *interdependent*, rather than *independent*, attributes that bear evidence of the work of the Spirit of God in the life of the Christian. In this book we will explore the relationship between Christian character and Christ-like conduct. As believers we are challenged to live victorious and incarnational lives. Dynamic Spirit-filled lives testify to the reality of resurrection power and thereby glorify God.

It is important to note that the passage speaks of 'fruit' and not fruits. Fruit may be singular or plural in the same way as words like 'fish' and 'sheep'. From the context, however, it is clear that what is being encouraged here is not that the believer should manifest some of these qualities but that they go together in a holistic sense.

Co-operating in divine activity

The Holy Spirit does not coerce believers to behave in a manner that is consistent with their beliefs. Rather the Holy Spirit convinces us intellectually and convicts us spiritually so that we desire to co-operate with his divine activity in our lives. Although we are not compelled or constrained to modify our attitudes or actions, the process of maturing that has commenced ought to continue as we yield to that divine authority in our lives. The Spirit is not only to reside in our hearts but also ought to reign there. The Spirit is to be sovereign rather than subordinate in our intellects, emotions and wills. We need to be submissive to the divine will and reliant on divine power so that God works in harmony with the regenerate human heart.

A healthy tree in its annual cycle will have foliage, flowers and fruit. One obvious means of identifying a tree is to see it bearing a particular kind of fruit. An apple tree bears apples; a pear tree bears pears and so on. Fruit is an organic part of the life of the tree. Although it is beautiful to look at, and it certainly enhances the appearance of the tree, fruit is not merely decorative.

I remember from my childhood the huge apple tree in the garden at home. It is not that I have come to mythologize the past so that nostalgia has caused the tree to be bigger in my memory than it was in reality. I have photographs of a garden party where my friends and I climbed up that old tree. It is, therefore, seen in true proportion and it remains the biggest and most bountiful apple tree I have ever seen. I remember too that a neighbour had an identical tree in type and size. Obviously the soil suited the growth of these spectacular specimens. But something else stands out in my mind about those two trees that is both interesting and relevant to our theme. Whereas our tree bore big, green, juicy, sweet apples the neighbour's tree bore smaller and less tasty fruit. Although I claim no horticultural expertise I can think of two reasons why that was so.

The first is that whereas our tree was situated in a cultivated garden the neighbour's tree was situated in a garden that was never tended and consequently overgrown. My father grew vegetables and we also had other fruit-bearing bushes such as red currants and gooseberries. My father never intentionally managed that old apple tree by pruning it or treating it with pesticide. But I believe that in taking care of the little things in the garden such as weeding, liming against slugs and digging in manure to fertilise the soil, the tree benefited from a healthy environment and produced a good crop. Here is a lesson that has a bearing on our exploration of the fruit of the Spirit. If we tend to the little things in 'love, joy, peace, patience, kindness, goodness, faithfulness, gentleness and self-control' then fruit will thrive. However, if we neglect the little things and allow the garden to become overrun then that will affect the quality of the fruit. My father's garden was free from pests and disease and that was beneficial to the production of fruit.

The second reason why our apple tree was bountiful relates to the first. The neighbour's garden was so overgrown that the weeds actually formed a canopy that blocked a lot of light from getting to his tree. It was always in shade and never in sunshine. Because my father tended his garden there was plenty of light getting through to our tree. Plants need light and people need light. A tree converts light through its foliage in the process of photosynthesis into energy that sustains its life and health. Similarly, the Christian needs the light of the Word of God illuminating his life for health and happiness. Without that light the tree will struggle to be what it ought to be. As we approach Scripture each day it is not enough to make observations and interpretations of that Word. We must seek the application of that Word in our lives. The light must penetrate to the heart of our spiritual lives and through that process of spiritual photosynthesis produce that vital divine energy needed for bearing fruit to the glory of God.

I recall that apple tree in our garden with its boughs bending under the weight of clusters of juicy apples. I never think of that apple tree as dutifully fulfilling its obligation to bear apples! Each spring it clothed itself in leaves, burst into bloom in summer and bore fruit in autumn.

Accepting all of the Spirit's graces

We have no liberty to pick and choose what virtues we will seek to nurture in our spiritual lives. We cannot, for example, say: 'I am not a very *patient* person but I can show *kindness* so I will focus on that instead'. These fruit taken together, sum up the nature of mature Christian character. The colours that compose light are seen only when that light is refracted as in a rainbow or a crystal prism. Together they provide vital illumination on everything else. We may speak of the fruit of the Spirit as nine separate qualities but in reality they form a unit that affects everything else around us.

Another important observation we need to make at this point is that the text refers to these graces as the fruit of the *Spirit* not the fruit of the *spirit*. This is crucial to our understanding of the text. These verses tell what the Holy Spirit may produce in the lives of Christ's disciples and not what we may summon up from within our own resources. It cannot therefore be about playing to our strengths and ignoring our weaknesses, so that we opt for kindness because we feel we can be kind but ignore patience because we feel we are just not wired that way. It is God who is at work in us to produce all of these qualities so that we may reflect and represent the true nature of the one whose noble name we bear as Christians.

Communion with God

Throughout this work we will seek to explain the meaning of these wonderful virtues and examine biblical examples that illustrate these qualities. That is the easy part. It is then up to us, with God's Spirit, to see these graces appropriated in our lives. I pray that by God's grace this work will provide sufficient clarity and inspiration to make a difference for our good and God's glory. The fruit of the Spirit is the outcome of unhurried daily communion with God where we are continuously being changed into his likeness: 'And we ... are being transformed into his likeness with ever-increasing glory, which comes from the Lord, who is the Spirit' (2 Corinthians 3:18). This is God's ultimate purpose for the believer as Paul explains to the Romans, 'For those God foreknew he also predestined to be conformed to the likeness of his Son' (Romans 8:29).

Being in the presence of God has an effect upon us that is obvious to others even if we are unaware of it ourselves. It is instructive for us to recall the occasion when Moses came down from Mount Sinai with the commandments. Thus in Exodus we read: 'When Moses came down from Mount Sinai with the two tablets of the Testimony in his hands, he was not aware that his face was radiant because he had spoken with the LORD. When Aaron and all the Israelites saw Moses, his face was radiant...' (34:29–30).

Some years ago I took my family on a holiday to Donegal in Ireland where we had two weeks of glorious sunshine. However, the rest of the country was experiencing very different weather. In the evenings when we watched the news on television we could hardly believe what we saw, cattle stranded in flooded fields, sheep that had drowned, crops ruined, river-embankments burst and homes flooded. It was awful and truly amazing that we had escaped such terrible conditions. During that holiday we spent our days on a little beach swimming, sunbathing, playing games and reading. One of the results of this time of rest and recreation was that when we returned home it was evident we had been in the sunshine. People wondered if we had been on a foreign holiday! I relate this not to illustrate the obvious point that if you spend time in the sun it will be apparent to others, but to point out that if we spend time with the Son we will radiate something of him.

In Acts 4 we read of Peter and John being taken before the Sanhedrin for preaching the gospel and verse 13 tells us something very interesting. There we read: 'When they saw the courage of Peter and John and realized that they were unschooled, ordinary men, they were astonished and they took note that these men had been with Jesus'. Both their courage and knowledge are identified as traits associated with the character and influence of Jesus. Thus it is with the fruit of the Spirit, which are evidences of the companionship and communion of Christ. Such graces advance harmony and unity in the church and testify to the watching world that God has given something special to his people. As such the fruit of the Spirit assists our proclamation of the message of the gospel by enabling us to live out the reality of God's grace in our homes, workplaces, colleges and communities. If we want to be effective in evangelism we must attend to this area of our life in the Spirit.

Exhibiting the values of the kingdom

In a book[1] on the fruit of the Spirit a story is related of the missionary John Hess Yoder who uses an analogy that illustrates a great kingdom truth.

While serving as a missionary in Laos, I discovered an illustration of the kingdom of God.

Before the colonialists imposed national boundaries, the kings of Laos and Vietnam reached an agreement on taxation in the border areas. Those who ate short-grain rice, built their houses on stilts, and decorated them with Indian-style serpents were considered Laotians. On the other hand, those who ate long-grain rice, built their houses on the ground and decorated them with Chinese-style dragons were considered Vietnamese.

The exact location of a person's home was not what determined his or her nationality. Instead each person belonged to the kingdom whose cultural values he or she exhibited.

The point is well illustrated that Christians do not belong to this world and as citizens of heaven must exhibit the values of the kingdom of God.

Integrity influences others

As we seek to persuade people of the truth and efficacy of the gospel we need to bear some things in mind. Firstly, the word 'persuade' means to cause a person to believe, to convince or to induce. Clearly it is only the power of the Holy Spirit that can prevail on people to believe. Secondly, for the Christian, believing, means more than giving intellectual assent to doctrine. It has to be more than merely acknowledging the veracity of truth because in James we read, 'You believe that there is one God. Good! Even the demons believe that—and shudder' (2:19). It is possible that a person could be intellectually convinced of the soundness of an argument and even be convicted of his or her condition before God and yet not be converted. Thirdly, and most importantly for our purposes, there has to be a credible connection between what we proclaim and what we practice. If our belief and behaviour are not consistent then we bring the gospel into disrepute. Our lives must be consistent with our message if we are to have credibility.

Ancient Greek and Roman civilisation was devoted to the dynamics of public speaking. Plato, Aristotle, Cicero and others contributed to the development of the rhetorical art form. Aristotle's seminal work, *Rhetoric*, was the standard text for the times. Aristotle had a particular genius for systematising knowledge and in this work he categorises the rhetorical art of persuasion in three divisions. Firstly, he deals with *ethos*, which focuses on the integrity of the speaker. Secondly, he deals with *logos*, which is about the inherent logic of the message itself. Thirdly, he deals with *pathos*, which is about the emotions evoked by the oration. Aristotle asserted that *ethos* (the integrity of the speaker) was the most significant and influential constituent in the rhetorical art of persuasion.

We can see certain parallels between this Aristotelian contribution to rhetorical analysis and the Christian. The integrity of those who desire to commend Christ, the authority of the Word and the appeal to emotions are all relevant factors in communicating Christ. However, we would want to stress the authority of the Word above the others (*ethos* and *pathos*). Firstly, because the Word of God (logos) quickens the souls of men: and secondly, because God may use a man in conveying the message of the gospel despite his deficiencies (*ethos*). We would also like to emphasise that the appeal of

Scripture (whether to the converted or unconverted) is to the intellect, emotions and will (*pathos* plus!).

Nevertheless, we cannot underestimate the importance of the integrity of the believer. His moral character may influence how the message itself is perceived. Augustine said, 'The life of the speaker has greater weight in determining whether he is obediently heard than any grandness of eloquence'.[2] Certainly a lack of integrity undermines credibility. Thus there is a connection between proclamation and practice insofar as the moral stature of the messenger contributes to enhancing the reception of the message. In short, people are more likely to heed what they hear from messengers with the kind of integrity manifested through the fruit of the Spirit.

When Paul says 'the fruit of the Spirit is love, joy, peace, patience, kindness, goodness, faithfulness, gentleness and self-control', he is giving us a profile of the Christian character rather than a finished portrait. Although it is not a comprehensive list[3] it is as commendable to us in our generation as it was to the Galatians in theirs. In a sense, as we shall see, here is holiness honed down to its essential features. God's purposes are fulfilled not only in our salvation which brings glory to God, but in our sanctification which also brings glory to God. Christ died for us but he also lived for us a life that perfectly demonstrated the fruit of the Spirit and in so doing set an example for us to follow. When we look at this list of graces we are forced to conclude that it is essential to emphasise the importance of this text in today's context.

What is fruit and what is the purpose of fruit?

Fruit is the seed-bearing part of a tree or plant. It is in fact the ovary, enclosing its seed(s). The principal botanical purpose of fruit is the protection and dissemination of that seed. There is an interesting parallel between the botanical and spiritual functions of fruit. In the horticultural sense fruit is primarily a seed-bearing container that is designed to protect the seed and ensure the multiplication of that species of seed-bearing plant. Fruit is a very efficient means of ensuring the dispersal of seed. The flesh of the fruit is a reserve of nutrient material that gives the new generation an excellent growing start. It acts as an effective layer of flesh that enables the seed to survive seasons of stress such as winter.

Introduction

As we have noted the fruit of the Spirit is the fruit of the Holy Spirit. This has profound implications for understanding and applying the Word in our lives. We are not, therefore, talking about the *spirit* of man but the *Spirit* of God. As such these virtues are not merely the result of something that emerges from within our own nature. God plants the seed of the Holy Spirit within the hearts of those whom he draws to himself in faith and repentance. Thus the impregnated heart has confessed its need of forgiveness and trusts in the completed work of Christ at Calvary. Although mankind has been generated by God in that act of creation recorded in the book of Genesis and naturally perpetuated through the procreative means ordained by God, he is dead spiritually and needs to be regenerated through the power of God. This happens when God impregnates the hearts of people with the seed of his Word, which brings forth the fruit of salvation and sanctification.

Pure or poisoned fruit

Every person bears fruit of one kind or another. The unregenerate person is controlled by his sinful nature and bears fruit in accordance with that nature. Paul contrasts walking in the flesh with walking in the Spirit in Galatians 5. He identifies a lifestyle that is contrary to that produced by the Spirit of God. Thus we read, 'the acts of the sinful nature are obvious: sexual immorality, impurity and debauchery; idolatry and witchcraft; hatred, discord, jealousy, fits of rage, selfish ambition, dissensions, factions and envy; drunkenness, orgies, and the like. I warn you, as I did before, that those who live like this will not inherit the kingdom of God' (Galatians 5:19–21). Here he is talking about people who habitually live like this and refuse to repent. Such people are not born of the Spirit, and people who profess to be Christians and continually engage in such practices are not, in fact, believers at all. The reality of the believer's new life is seen in the fruit of the Spirit. It is not that the believer never sins rather he has a heart that is tender to the things of God, repentant when sin is committed and open to the influence of the Holy Spirit. Although the Christian always retains the capacity to sin, the inclination diminishes and the pleasure of sin becomes sour and unpalatable.

It is only the regenerate who can bear the fruit of the Holy Spirit. As the apostle Paul stated in his letter to the Romans: 'So, my brothers, you also died to the law through the body of Christ, that you might belong to another, to him who was raised from the dead, in order that we might bear fruit to God. For when we were controlled by the sinful nature, the sinful passions aroused by the law were at work in our bodies, so that we bore fruit for death. But now, by dying to what once bound us, we have been released from the law so that we serve in the new way of the Spirit, and not in the old way of the written code' (7:4–6).

Unregenerate mankind may bear faint traces of the likeness of God in his fallen spirit[4] and can manifest love, joy, peace, patience, kindness, goodness, faithfulness, gentleness and self-control in some measure and even to a very significant degree. It would be entirely churlish to deny this. Nevertheless, it is only in the life of those who have been regenerated by the Spirit of God that these fruit are truly manifest as God intended. One might object to such a statement and say that surely every human being knows what it is to love and be loved, and to know joy and peace in their lives. they should recognise these qualities as desirable and aspire toward achieving such moral ideals. One could well say that surely it is not only Christians who are patient, kind and good and that the followers of Christ do not have a monopoly on faithfulness, gentleness and self-control. In fact one could point to many Christians who do not manifest such qualities to an admirable degree. Sadly we admit that we are not what we should be, but we also thank God that we are not what we were and we are becoming what God wants us to be.

Stealing God's glory

The reality is that many people who have been loving, kind, patient, peace-loving and so on, are remembered and revered for such traits themselves and do not bring glory to God. Martin Luther in his commentary on Galatians said that the disciples of Jesus 'bring with them most excellent fruits and maximum usefulness, for they that have them give glory to God, and with the same do allure and provoke others to embrace the doctrine and faith of Christ.'[5] The fruit of the Spirit is not only for our good; it is also and ultimately for the glory of the Almighty. Conversion may not *instantly* produce such fruit but it should *eventually*.

Introduction

Spiritual perspective

Can *love* ever be fully understood without a true spiritual comprehension of the love of God, particularly as it was displayed in time and history at Calvary? Is it possible to experience true *joy* without being in a right relationship with God? How can any person know the real meaning of *peace* and experience the true value of it if they are not first at peace *with* God? It is from this harmonious relationship of life lived in reverence for God (as it was intended) that the peace *of* God, which transcends all understanding, might be known. It is in knowing the *patience, kindness, goodness, faithfulness, gentleness and self-control* of God appropriated in our lives through mercy and grace that we come to see these virtues in their true light. Then it is out of such experiential, albeit partial, knowledge that the fruit of the Spirit is made manifest.

Improvement and reproduction

In the horticultural world, in general, the chief concerns of those engaged in fruit cultivation are the propagation and improvement of varieties of fruit. Similarly in the spiritual realm, amongst believers, there is a desire for improvement and reproduction. Natural fruit grows in a certain season and in specific climatic and soil conditions that are favourable to the success of the crop. In the spiritual realm the fruit of the Spirit is more likely to be evidenced in the life of the mature believer. The new believer is like a freshly planted sapling apple tree. The prevailing soil conditions or the environment in which the young Christian finds himself will have an effect on his development. If the soil is rich in nutrient material and the sapling believer is being fed by the Word of God and well watered in prayer, this will have a positive outcome on his growth to maturity. In the spring of that new life branches will bear buds and leaves will unfurl. Just as the leaves of a plant absorb sunlight for its benefit, so the light of God's Word when absorbed (understood and applied) develops the believer. As the sapling grows it will come into a summer season of splendid growth. As summer passes it develops beautiful blossoms and autumn turns those pretty flowers to little apples that grow and grow. There is a connection between the root and the fruit insofar as those who are grounded in the Word of God will grow to be healthy and strong and fruit will be the outcome. As the psalmist put it, 'Blessed is the man who does not walk in the counsel of the wicked or stand in the way of sinners or sit in the seat of mockers. But his delight is in the law of the LORD, and on his law he meditates day and night. He is like a tree planted by streams of water, which yields its fruit in season and whose leaf does not wither' (Psalm 1:1–3).

Tending the garden

The fruit of the Spirit is not to be confused with the gifts of the Spirit. With regard to the gifts we may say that any particular believer ought not to expect to have all the gifts. However, with regard to the fruit of the Spirit every Christian should expect to have all the fruit listed in their lifestyle. All believers, young and old, should manifest the fruit of the Spirit just as young apple trees and old apple trees bear apples. Nevertheless there may be a season in the life of the believer that is part of the process of producing fruit, when that fruit is not evident. This is not to justify the absence of such fruit but to encourage the genuine believer who desires to see more of that fruit in his life. Do not be discouraged. Rather ask yourself, are the soil conditions favourable to producing that fruit? Are you feeding on the Word of God? Are you well irrigated in prayer?

The great gardener may need to prune the sapling. It is his technique for ensuring healthy development by correcting unhealthy development. The church too must labour to ensure the best soil management, irrigation, and pest control so that the tender shoot may grow to maturity in Christ. In the spiritual world, just as in the horticultural world, there are pests that threaten to damage or destroy the development of the fruit-bearing plant/person. With regard to spiritual pests the best approach to healthy development is the same as that in the horticultural world, i.e. preventative measures are better than remedial action but both strategies will inevitably need to be employed.

Sacred seed

We have already stated that fruit is the seed-bearing part of a tree or plant and that its primary function is to protect the seed and facilitate its dispersal and dissemination. But what exactly is the similarity between the function of ordinary fruit and the purpose of spiritual fruit? When God puts his Spirit in human hearts he makes provision for that sacred seed to be enveloped in 'love, joy, peace, patience, kindness, goodness, faithfulness, gentleness and self-control'. This effective covering acts as a barrier that prevents external conditions (opposition, ridicule, rejection, imprisonment, torture and death) from destroying that seed. Just as in the natural realm God has designed seed for the purpose of propagating the species, so in the spiritual realm God desires that the precious seed of his Word be dispersed in a manner conducive to its positive reception leading to the regeneration of others.

This is particularly evident in the Christian home where the new generation is given an excellent growing start by being surrounded by that reserve of nutrient material ('love, joy, peace, patience, kindness, goodness, faithfulness, gentleness and self-control'). This enables them to survive the inevitable seasons of stress encountered in the Christian life and in turn carry that seed to hearts cultivated by God as receptive repositories where that precious seed may again germinate, take root and grow to bear fruit for the glory of God.

Healthy hearts

In the natural world, fruit and the seeds they contain are hugely important economically, primarily because they are sources of a variety of foods. In the spiritual realm the fruit of the Spirit is of immense value to the wellbeing of the church. Consider how the fruit of the Spirit in its splendid variety provides nourishment for hungry souls. Love, joy, peace, patience, kindness, goodness, faithfulness, gentleness and self-control are evidence of the existence of the Holy Spirit in the life of the believer. Moreover they provide the perfect conditions for the healthy development of church life. Such fruit is the rich nutrient material that sustains healthy and happy relationships within the church and furthermore it is the attractive substance that entices hungry souls.

There are things that grieve the Holy Spirit and we must do all that we can to prevent this from happening. Paul gives this advice: 'do not grieve the Holy Spirit of God, with whom you were sealed for the day of redemption' (Ephesians 4:30). He is cautioning us to avoid offending God. We might well ask; what is it that offends God? The answer is sin! Sin in all its manifestations is an affront to the Almighty.

A cluster of Christ-like characteristics

We have already stated that these fruit are more *interdependent* than *independent*. For example if there were more *love* all the other graces listed would flow from it in abundance. If there were more *patience* there would be greater *self-control* (and vice-versa) and *peace* would prevail and so on. The desire for the fruit of the Spirit should be such that it would characterise our personal and corporate prayer. Our desire is to be like Jesus who manifested these fruit in abundance.

Fruitlessness condemned

It is instructive for us to recall the account of Christ and the incident with the fig tree in Matthew's gospel where we read these words: 'Early in the morning, as he was on his way back to the city, he was hungry. Seeing a fig tree by the road, he went up to it but found nothing on it, except leaves. Then he said to it, "May you never bear fruit again!" Immediately the tree withered' (Matthew 21:18–19). What are we to make of this? Does this incident show some kind of flaw in Christ's character? Is it to be understood as an 'intemperate outburst' like the occasion when he overthrew tables and whipped those who were trading in the outer courts of the temple area?[6] Certainly not! Neither occasion has anything to do with loss of self-control. In this incident concerning the fig tree Christ is coming as creator to his creation and he desires the fruit it was intended to bear. It is a source of disappointment to Jesus that the fig tree is barren. He leaves us in no doubt that such an object is worthless. May it never be that God would come to us, as his new creation in Christ, looking for the fruit of the Holy Spirit and not find any! If we are barren in this regard then we too are useless and we disappoint the heart of God.

Being effective and productive

Every true disciple of Jesus desires to be an effective and productive Christian. To be effective and productive is to be fruitful and to be ineffective and unproductive is to be unfruitful. When the believer lacks the fruit of the Spirit he is impotent. Thus Peter expresses this thought in his second epistle: 'For this very reason, make every effort to add to your faith goodness; and to goodness, knowledge; and to knowledge, self-control; and to self-control, perseverance; and to perseverance, godliness; and to godliness, brotherly kindness; and to brotherly kindness, love. For if you possess these qualities in increasing measure, they will keep you from being ineffective and unproductive in your knowledge of our Lord Jesus Christ. But if anyone does not have them, he is short-sighted and blind, and has forgotten that he has been cleansed from his past sins' (2 Peter 1:5–9). If we are to be powerful and prolific people in a spiritual sense then we must display the fruit of the Spirit.

A difference in kind

We have already stated that it would be churlish to suggest that people outside of Christ know nothing of the qualities listed in chapter five of Galatians as 'the fruit of the Spirit', but we need to say a little more on this point. The non-Christian could equally well accuse believers of their shortcomings with regard to these virtues. All people, Christian and non-Christian, have a capacity for love, joy, peace and so on. God the creator has given that potential to everyone. It is not that such capability inherent in the individual lies dormant until the seed of the Holy Spirit impregnates the person. Rather it is that the full potential of the person to experience and exhibit such qualities cannot ever be realised outside of Christ. The non-Christian may protest but we would counter that by saying what they know to be love is not measured by the ultimate standard of love. We would say that what the world calls peace is a poor thing in comparison to the peace God gives in Christ and so on. Perhaps the point could be illustrated like this: a life-sized cardboard cut-out of a person is a convincing image of that person but it is infinitely less and indeed entirely other than the three-dimensional reality of that person's presence. It may be lifelike insofar as it closely resembles the person represented. Nevertheless it is, in fact, lifeless. It is dead and unconscious and lacking movement and vitality. Even where the image is animated, say for example, in a video or DVD, it is still only an image of reality. There is not just a qualitative difference between the picture and the person. Rather there is a difference in kind.

Don't be discouraged

It ought to be evident by now that we, as Christians, fall far short of what we should be. If we are honest we will admit that desire and determination to be Christ-like in manifesting the fruit of the Spirit have, in themselves, proved to be inadequate. Desire and determination must be assisted by the divine grace of God. It is easy for the sensitive believer to become discouraged and disheartened, to feel that he is not living up to the standard and there must be something wrong with him. Nevertheless we do not lose hope as we strive for the goal forgetting that which is behind. We can measure ourselves against others and feel like failures or even quite self-righteous. But when we measure ourselves against Christ we realise that there is no place for smugness. We do not accuse one another of failure; rather we encourage each other towards a better future. The sensitive and sincere believer may look around and imagine that others have this fruit in abundance while he is barren. It may be true that people who are mature in Christ and are bearing the fruit of the Spirit surround him, but he should not think that others are free from the inclination and habit of sin.

Every disciple of Christ is tempted and every Christian has trials at one point or another in his life. Every believer has struggles and issues to grapple with (admittedly some more than others) and any honest believer will readily admit this. We all have a propensity to sin and selfishness that runs counter to God's will but we do not become defeatist. The devil tells us we are no good and in that much he is telling the truth. But our God is good and our God is great and it is by his sovereign and inscrutable decree that we are unconditionally elected to salvation. We are neither saved nor sanctified by our good deeds. This does not mean that we become reckless and abuse our liberty in Christ by using it as a licence to gratify our own sinful desires and ignore our obligations. Rather it means that when Satan points that accusing finger at us we can point to grace, amazing grace! Christ does not accuse us. Certainly the Holy Spirit may convince us of truth, convict us of sin and prompt us to holy living but the Spirit of God does not condemn us. Rather it is consciousness of our great debt of gratitude to God for his infinite grace that stimulates us to manifest 'love, joy, peace, patience, kindness, goodness, faithfulness, gentleness and self-control'.

The key to fruitfulness

The key to Christ's fruitful life is his union and communion with the Father. For example, Luke tells us that 'Jesus often withdrew to lonely places and prayed' (5:16). Frequent and fervent prayer indicates the reality of dynamic spiritual relationship. Jesus spoke about the intimate and organic nature of the relationship his disciples ought to have with him when he said 'I am the vine; you are the branches. If a man remains in me and I in him, he will bear much fruit ...' (John 15:5). Fruitfulness is found in Christ and we are dependent on him for such grace in our lives. The key to our fruitfulness depends on the quality of our relationship with Jesus. This means spending time in prayer and meditation of the Scriptures.

Clarifying our approach

Finally, we need to clarify our approach to the text of Galatians 5:22–23. There is obviously a difference in the English translations between the listing of the fruit of the Spirit in the *New International Version* of the Bible (NIV) and the *Authorised Version* of the Bible (AV). We have referred to the NIV throughout this work for several reasons. Firstly, the AV refers to *'patience'* as *'longsuffering'* which is a marvellous word to convey the true sense of the meaning of patience but it is a word that is no longer in common usage today. Secondly, we deal with *'kindness'* (as listed in the NIV text) and not *'gentleness'* (as listed in the AV). The word in Greek is *chréstotés*, which means 'kindness or goodness of heart'. It is a noun and the corresponding adjective *chréstos* is translated 'good', 'kind', 'easy', 'gracious'. It seems, therefore, that the word *'kindness'* conveys the original and intended meaning better than *'gentleness'*. Thirdly, when we come to consider *'faith'* (AV) or *'faithfulness'* (NIV) it seems best to take into account the implications of both. They are connected in such a way that to take either to the exclusion of the other would restrict us in gaining the fullest understanding of the text. Fourthly, the fruit listed in the AV as *'meekness'* is listed in the NIV as *'gentleness'* because it is associated with the Greek word *enkrateia,* which means 'self-control'. *'Meekness'*, however, has a deeper meaning than that which is generally understood with the word *'gentleness'*. We will, therefore, explain that meaning by including the AV's use of *'meekness'* in chapter nine. Fifthly, there is no major difference between the NIV rendition of 'self-control' and the AV interpretation, 'temperance' except perhaps that 'temperance' is sometimes associated in people's minds in a restricted sense as abstinence from alcohol consumption. We feel it is best therefore to cover the broader sense here represented by the phrase 'self-control'.

We cannot know the fruit that comes from walking in the Spirit unless we fully surrender our lives to Christ. Although we may know some measure of love, joy, peace and so on we will never enter fully into fruitfulness if we reserve areas of our lives that are deemed out of bounds for the Spirit's government.

We trust that fuller understanding of the meaning of the verses will lead to a greater appreciation and application of the Word of God for our personal good, the good of others and God's glory.

In *Knowing and Doing the Will of God*, J.I. Packer says:

'Love is the Christlike reaction to people's malice.

Joy is the Christlike reaction to depressing circumstances.

Peace is the Christlike reaction to troubles, threats and invitations to anxiety.

Patience is the Christlike reaction to all that is maddening.

Kindness is the Christlike reaction to all that is unkind.

Goodness is the Christlike reaction to bad people and bad behaviour.

Faithfulness and gentleness are the Christlike reactions to lies and fury.

Self-control is the Christlike reaction to every situation that goads you to lose your cool and hit out.[7]

The fruit of the Spirit is Christ-likeness and we are called to the challenge of cultivating Christian character in a corrupt, carnal and cynical world. Let us, therefore, walk in the Spirit and glorify God. In a world that presents us with many challenges the Christian who is bearing the fruit of the Spirit can make a real difference.

Working for God's glory and our good

It is in the overall context of the delivery of advice to the church in Galatia that the fruit of the Spirit is listed as the ideal virtues that ought to attend those who walk in the Spirit. We must not think of it as human advice since Paul is merely the agent of the Holy Spirit in writing this instruction to the Galatian believers. It is imperative that in this age of non-directive counselling we get hold of the idea that these words are not a 'take it if you like and leave it if you don't' kind of advice. Paul, rather, is directing believers, not just the Galatians then and there but all believers subsequently (including us) in the here and now. Paul has been talking about freedom in Christ and how the Christian has been liberated from the consequences of the law. It is clear from his advice to this troubled church that there are obligations attendant upon such freedom. The Galatian church had become legalistic but Paul called them back to grace. Nevertheless the central message of this text, 'But the fruit of the Spirit is love, joy, peace, patience, kindness, goodness, faithfulness, gentleness and self-control' (Galatians 5:22–23) is that where the Holy Spirit resides and reigns there will be bountiful evidence of his indwelling presence. Furthermore this outworking of the Spirit's inner existence will have profound implications for the life of the individual, the church and society at large. There is, without doubt, a social dimension to the fruit of the Spirit. 'Love, joy, peace, patience, kindness, goodness, faithfulness, gentleness and self-control' are virtues that ennoble and transform relationships. It must be pointed out that we should derive our understanding of the nature of such qualities from the Word of God and not accept the world's devalued definitions and descriptions of these virtues.

Notes to Introduction

1 **Thomas E. Trask and Wayde I. Goodall,** The Fruit of the Spirit: Becoming the Person God Wants You to Be (Zondervan, 2000), p. 20. The authors are quoting **Craig Brian Larson,**

Illustrations for Preaching and Teaching from Leadership Journal (Grand Rapids, Baker, 1993), p. 55.

2 *On Christian Doctrine,* 4.27.59.

3 The list of nine fruit does not include other biblical virtues such as contentment, courage, honesty, humility, and purity, to name some.

4 I am not denying the total depravity of man, as I am not asserting that there is anything meritorious in our fallen nature.

5 **Martin Luther,** *Commentary on Galatians* (Modern-English edition, Revell, Grand Rapids, 1998), p.378.

6 The incident in the temple is discussed more fully in chapter nine.

7 Quoted in **Thomas E. Trask and Wayde I. Goodall,** *The Fruit of the Spirit: Becoming the Person God Wants You to Be,* (Zondervan, Grand Rapids, Michigan, 2000), p. 78.

Love

'But the fruit of the Spirit is love …'

The context

Before we go on to examine the biblical definition of love we should note that Paul is seeking to teach the Galatians about the work of the Holy Spirit in the Christian life. Earlier he had spoken to them of the work of the Spirit in conversion: 'Are you so foolish? After beginning with the Spirit, are you now trying to attain your goal by human effort?' (Galatians 3:3). The Holy Spirit seeks to bring about that transformational life by working through the intellect, emotions and will of the individual Christian. It is nevertheless, the work of the Spirit of God and not merely human endeavour, which will ultimately produce such qualities. So it is out of a life that is inhabited and influenced by the Holy Spirit that such fruit organically develops.

What is love?

It is significant that the list of the fruit of the Spirit begins with *love* as it is not only first in position but foremost in priority. Love is a powerful force and in biblical terms it is something that will endure forever. We now come to outline a proper understanding of *love*. In order to do this we need to take our keynote from the Bible. The world's understanding of the nature of love is either inaccurate or inadequate because people in their sinful condition, estranged from God and at enmity with God, cannot have a truly spiritual perspective on this issue.

Some people who profess to be Christians are confused about Christian love, as they seem to think that anybody who loves is a child of God. Certainly John says, 'Everyone who loves has been born of God' (1 John 4:7), but in the same epistle (which must be taken as a whole unit) he says that there must be corroborating evidence of belonging to God. In chapter three, for example, he says 'No-one who is born of God will continue to sin'

(v. 9). This suggests that an obedient and holy life demonstrates kinship with Christ. In chapter five he says, 'Everyone who believes that Jesus is the Christ is born of God' (v. 1) and this clearly means that believing in Jesus' sacrificial and sufficient death identifies an individual as belonging to God.

There are three Greek words that refer to the concept of love. Firstly, there is the word *phileo* from which we get the word philosophy, which is a composite of two Greek words, *phileo* and *sophia*. *Phileo* means 'love' and *sophia* means 'wisdom'. Hence the word philosophy means love of wisdom. This is a platonic love, which is used in the context of friendship and companionship. Jesus uses the word *phileo* in John 15:19 where he says that those who belong to him will not be loved by the world. Secondly, the Greek word for sexual love is *eros* from which we get the English word 'erotic'. It speaks of a desire for gratification. Thirdly, we have the word *agape* and this is the word that is used to describe the love of God for us, and the kind of love he expects from us. *Agape* is a selfless love that is not contingent upon conditions and reciprocation. This is the kind of love Jesus speaks of when he speaks of the love between him and his heavenly Father (John 15:9–13). It is also the kind of love he expects to prevail within the family of God. In fact he commands it: 'this is my command: Love each other' (John 15:17).

There have been many great works of literature (poetic, dramatic and prosaic) based on the theme of love but I would argue that the greatest description or definition of love ever written is located in 1 Corinthians 13. It is a passage of Scripture that is often read at wedding services and for all its familiarity within the Christian tradition spanning two millennia it has endured the test of time. It is still potent enough to induce goose pimples, making one feel that the quality of their love falls far short of the ideal it upholds and stirs one's heart to greater resolve to love better in the future. Because the Holy Spirit is describing and defining love in this passage and because we are seeking to gain insight into 'love' as fruit of the Spirit, it is important to take a close look at this passage of Scripture.

If I speak in the tongues of men and of angels, but have not love, I am only a resounding gong or a clanging cymbal. If I have the gift of prophecy and can fathom all mysteries and all knowledge, and if I have a faith that can move mountains, but have not love, I am nothing. If I give all I possess to the poor and surrender my body to the flames, but have not love, I gain nothing.

Love is patient, love is kind. It does not envy, it does not boast, it is not proud. It is not rude, it is not self-seeking, it is not easily angered, it keeps no record of wrongs. Love does not delight in evil but rejoices with the truth. It always protects, always trusts, always hopes, always perseveres.

Love never fails. But where there are prophecies, they will cease; where there are tongues, they will be stilled; where there is knowledge, it will pass away ...

And now these three remain: faith, hope and love. But the greatest of these is love (1 Corinthians 13:1–13).

Essentially this beautiful passage establishes the supremacy of love and the indispensable place it must have in the life of the church, which we do well to remember consists of individual believers. The great gifts that the Holy Spirit deigned to bestow on the church such as tongues, prophesy and discerning knowledge are nothing without love.

This chapter then goes on to describe the characteristics of love and encapsulates in such a short space the distilled essence of this supreme virtue. Love is not ephemeral; it is something that has an enduring quality. It is presented as greater than faith and hope!

This chapter really speaks for itself and no commentary can do it justice. However, we want to draw attention to some of its statements as they clarify the true nature of love. The word 'love' here is the Greek word *agape*, which is used in the New Testament for the deep and constant tenderness shared between the heavenly Father and Jesus. Jesus speaks of this abiding affection when he says, 'If you obey my commands, you will remain in my love, just as I have obeyed my Father's commands and remain in his love' (John 15:10). This abiding affection between the Father and the Son is reinforced in John 17. There in his great prayer Jesus says: 'I have made you known to them, and will continue to make you known in order that the love you have for me may be in them and that I myself may be in them' (John 17:26). God has this same *agape* love for us, and it is a love which was demonstrated in Christ's life and majestically displayed in his death. 'This is how God showed his love among us: he sent his one and only Son into the world that we might live through him' (1 John 4:9). But this word *agape* is also used with regard to how Christians ought to relate to each other. 'A new command I give you: Love one another. As I have loved you, so you must love one another. By this all men will know that you are my disciples, if you love one another' (John 13:34–35). *Agape* love is a love by choice and is different to *philos*, which is a love by chance. It is a love of the will and not just emotion.

It should be a natural outworking of the Christian faith to love one another because the 'Christian', as the name implies, belongs to God and Scripture tells us that 'God is love' (1 John 4:8). If God is love and if God the Holy Spirit possesses the heart of the believer then that fruit of love will ripen and become evident to all.

Having a healthy attitude

With regard to the passage from Paul's first epistle to the Corinthians we should say that love is the context for the proper operation of whatever gifts God has bestowed on the Christian in the local church. Apparently the Corinthians had lacked perspective and did not have a healthy attitude to the exercise of the gifts of the Spirit. They placed great emphasis on the gifts and seemed to have obvious shortcomings when it came to understanding and exercising love for Christ and their fellow Christians. It is quite frightening to think that one could exercise such gifts as tongues and prophecy without love. It is chilling to think that one could have great spiritual discernment and insight and yet lack love. Imagine having 'faith that can move mountains' and knowing nothing of love! If love is not the motive for giving all one's material wealth to the poor it amounts to nothing! Martyrdom is meaningless if it is not an act of love!

The Corinthian passage tells us what love is and also what love is not! Positively it describes love as 'patient'. Love waits without being frustrated and demonstrates an ability to endure delay, hardship and provocation. Love is characterised by perseverance and forbearance. Then it describes love as 'kind'. So it is something which might be identified by generous, gracious, compassionate and charitable characteristics.

Then negatively the passage continues to define love by contrasting it with attributes that are opposite to its essential nature such as envy, boastfulness, pride, rudeness, self-seeking and anger. These vices violate love! We learn from this portrait of love that true love does not harbour grudges and resentments. It takes no pleasure in anything wrong or bad. Rather it takes great joy in what is truthful and good. It is something that seeks to safeguard, and its instinct is to confidently believe. Love is optimistic and expectant. It is determined, steadfast, steady and resolute. It being all of that we soon come to realise why we need the power of the Holy Spirit to produce it within us.

As Christians we are both beneficiaries and benefactors of love. In our fallen nature we are essentially bankrupt, but God, the ultimate benefactor of love, invests in us through mercy and grace. It is out of such a vast deposit of love that we come to have reserves of love for God and for others. This is the fruit of the Spirit's work.

The Love of God

God's love for humanity is demonstrated in creation and his providential care. It is seen in the Old Testament in his patient, persistent, faithful and forgiving covenant relationship with a rebellious people. In the New Testament it is displayed in the incarnation, ministry and death of Jesus for a hostile people.

Love exists within the Godhead as Paul says to the Colossians, 'For he has rescued us from the dominion of darkness and brought us into the kingdom of the Son he loves, in whom we have redemption, the forgiveness of sins' (Colossians 1:13–14). This love is expressed at the baptism of Jesus when the voice from heaven said, 'This is my Son, whom I love; with him I am well pleased' (Matthew 3:17). We see love in action in the incarnation of Christ who condescended to be born into humanity in humble circumstances. It is this kind of Christ-likeness that Paul exhorts in Philippians:

Your attitude should be the same as that of Christ Jesus: who, being in very nature God, did not consider equality with God something to be grasped, but made himself nothing, taking the very nature of a servant, being made in human likeness. And being found in appearance as a man, he humbled himself and became obedient to death—even death on a cross! (2:5–8).

God's love for men is revealed in his ministry where there are numerous accounts of loving acts such as compassionate healing. God's love is about service and sacrifice and this ought to motivate us to love others through sacrificial service. Love is compassion in action. Love is an invisible quality made visible through action. Christ's ministry was one of reconciliation between the sinner and God through faith in him. We see how Christ was moved emotionally by the disobedience of people when he laments over Jerusalem: 'O Jerusalem, Jerusalem, you who kill the prophets and stone those sent to you, how often I have longed to gather your children together, as a hen gathers her chicks under her wings, but you were not willing' (Matthew 23:37). That love was expressed in his association with sinners. The event of redemption in the history of humanity as displayed in the death of Christ at Calvary is a dramatic delineation of God's immense love in action. As Paul put it to the Romans, 'God demonstrates his own love for us in this: while we were still sinners, Christ died for us' (Romans 5:8).

Love in action

Let us consider in some detail an incident that demonstrates the compassionate character of Christ. In Mark 1 we read of an incident in the life of Christ that reveals something special about his loving nature.

A man with leprosy came to him and begged him on his knees, 'If you are willing, you can make me clean.' Filled with compassion, Jesus reached out his hand and touched the man. 'I am willing,' he said. 'Be clean!' Immediately the leprosy left him and he was cured (Mark 1:40–42).

Here is the story of a leprous man who met the Lord and Master of mankind. He was a man with a serious and contagious disease of the skin that at its worst damaged nerves and caused disfigurement. The word 'leprosy' in the Bible refers to various dermatological disorders. We don't want to get hung up on technicalities, so suffice to say that whatever condition this man was in, it caused him to come to Christ and plead for cleansing. We do not know the full extent of the problem. He may have been hideously disfigured or not but we do know that as a leper, he was deemed to be unclean and as such he was an untouchable outcast from society.

This incident reveals the compassionate character of Christ. We see love in action. By focusing on it we see what Jesus did for that man and it stimulates us to think of what he has done for us through a loving touch. May it also inspire us to believe that his love can radically transform the lives of others, especially those that are rejected by society! Compassion is more than sorrow or pity. The *Pocket Oxford Dictionary* defines compassion as 'pity inclining one to help or be merciful'. Christ-like compassion brings to fruition that inclination to help. It is love reaching out!

This leprous man met the Lord and Master in his wretched and pitiful condition and begged him on his knees. Another gospel account tells us he 'fell with his face to the ground and begged him' (Luke 5:12). The posture this man assumes and the compassionate response of Jesus is an indication that the skin-disorder was nothing less than what we know as leprosy. The context makes it difficult to think of it as anything less and it is certainly not some kind of rash! It is reasonable to assume, therefore, that his condition was chronic. In fact Luke tells us that he was a man 'covered with leprosy' (5:12). It is worth bearing in mind that Luke was a physician and would have observed the detail very keenly indeed.

Leviticus 13 outlines regulations concerning infectious skin diseases. Leviticus 14 outlines the detailed regulations to be observed in relation to cleansing from infectious skin diseases. They relate to ceremonial cleansing (after a person has been examined by the priest) and after healing has taken place. In other words they were not a ritual cure! The Judaic law clearly stated: 'The person with such an infectious disease must wear torn clothes, let his hair be unkempt, cover the lower part of his face and cry out, "Unclean! Unclean!" As long as he has the infection he remains unclean. He must live alone; he must live outside the camp' (Leviticus 13:45–46). Yet this man came into the middle of a crowd and within arms length of Jesus.

The rejected need love

Here is a man who was shunned. Can you imagine the loneliness? Can you imagine the pain of separation, perhaps even from loved ones? There may very well have been a loss of livelihood. Imagine the awfulness of the absence of intimacy. Consider the damage to his self-esteem and confidence. Imagine the shame, the stigma, and the rejection. He lived either alone or with other lepers. It was a bleak situation. We do not know how long he was in that condition. He was obviously aware that his condition was beyond his control. It was bad enough for him to take desperate measures. That is what his coming to Christ is, an act of desperation conceived in hope.

To whom could he turn? There was no cure for leprosy. No physician could help him. To achieve a cure was a task beyond all human power. Lepers were quarantined from the community and so he was separated and segregated irrespective of family ties or occupational considerations. I wonder if he had heard of Jesus or perhaps seen him from a distance. Maybe the miracles of Jesus were a topic of conversation in the leper colony. Were they saddened that Jesus had not yet cured a leper? Nobody had cured a leper since the days of Elisha when Naaman was cured. That story would have been part of his traditional religious lore and perhaps it permitted this nameless man to allow hope to enter and grow in his heart. Although his identity is not known to us he is a real person and not a type invented for moral instruction. This is not a parable. He nurtured and cherished that hope until it grew into faith. So by the time we meet him in Mark 1:40 he is publicly acknowledging his faith in Christ with these words, 'If you are willing, you can make me clean.' He does not doubt that Christ *could* cure him but he cannot be certain if Christ *would* cure him.

Maybe he thought that Jesus would not even look upon him because he was loathsome. It is possible that many doctors, priests and teachers of the law had brushed him aside. We must remember that there is no record that this man had witnessed any miracle of the Master first-hand. There must have been rumours. We have the benefit of hindsight through the gospel accounts. He hadn't yet seen that divine compassion for himself. But he was about to experience the grace of God in his life. Jesus would look at him with eyes full of compassion and speak to him in a loving tone.

He didn't doubt that Jesus could help him but it remained to be seen if Jesus would help him. He could at least try; he had nothing to lose and everything to gain. However, there was one remaining difficulty; how could he gain access to Jesus? He couldn't go into the town to seek him. As a leper he was forbidden to enter the crowd that usually surrounded Jesus. But he could wait on the road to Capernaum. Imagine him waiting there alone and then the moment arrives. He hears the noise of a crowd and his heart pounds as Jesus approaches. The one who could deliver him from this horrible bondage is approaching. This leprous man comes up close to Jesus and drops on his knees and cries out, 'If you are willing, you can make me clean.' He had done it. How would Jesus respond? It probably felt as if the clock had stopped as he waited to hear from Jesus. But that agonising moment of suspense was very brief. There was no protracted delay. Our text says, 'Filled with compassion, Jesus reached out his hand and touched the man. "I am willing," he said. "Be clean!" Immediately the leprosy left him and he was cured' (Mark 1:41–42).

This man had acknowledged his own miserable condition. In coming to Christ he declared that he was ready to receive mercy and that Jesus was able to dispense it. He made a passionate appeal. There were no preliminaries, no introduction, no customary salutation or greeting. He came very directly to the point. He had one opportunity and he was determined not to miss it. He makes a very profound statement of faith. This man had grasped the very important truth that Jesus had the power and authority to make him well. In short he was saying: you can do it - will you?

Love doesn't make excuses

Look at the response of Christ. He did not say: 'I want you to learn from your suffering'. He did not say: 'curing one leper won't make much difference in a suffering world'. He did not say 'my mission is spiritual, not physical. Go to a physician'. He healed him. The master could have healed him with a word but he went beyond words and touched him! This is not an insignificant detail. Here is a man who had not been touched for some time; a man whose presence was detested by others. But Christ was filled with compassion. Whichever way we look at it he had compassion and used it powerfully, or he had power and used it compassionately. Jesus was 'moved' and issued a command that had all the force and authority of heaven. This miracle, like all miracles, demonstrates the power of God but it is also an important insight into the compassionate nature of God. The miracles authenticate his authority and validate his divine identity, but Jesus was not trying to prove his true identity by demonstrating his power. This was no public relations exercise designed to attract a greater following, in fact we learn from the rest of the account that Jesus wanted it hushed up. It is not that Christ had a motive in ministering to this man, it is simply that he was moved. He healed out of love for the sufferer.

Jesus touching this man would have shocked onlookers who knew of the ritual uncleanness of lepers. Jesus set him free out of love. It was compassion that expressed itself in a gracious deed. Although this is a story about physical healing there is a spiritual parallel in that this is what Christ has done for all sinners: 'He took up our infirmities and carried our diseases' (Matthew 8:17; Isaiah 53:4). What a beautiful story it is, such a tender outpouring of God's heart of love. His love is both compassionate and sacrificial. It is a love that we are called to demonstrate in a needy world.

Love in a look and touch

Imagine what it must have been like for this miserable man to look into the face of Jesus. Imagine what it must have been like for him to see such tenderness in those eyes. Can we even begin to understand the emotions he experienced when he felt the touch of Jesus' hand? He heard the words he desperately desired to hear and he must have heard them in a tone of voice saturated in love. It is ironic but it is enough to make us envy this leper! He had a hideous disease and was transformed in an instant because he threw himself upon the goodwill of Jesus and did not find him begrudging in dispensing bountiful grace. It is very unsatisfactory in life to depend on the goodwill of others for our happiness or wellbeing. Human love is fickle, frail and flawed but God's love is perfect. Perhaps you are conscious of your own great need and aware that only Jesus offers hope. Will you put yourself on the road where you can meet with Jesus and have that vital life-transforming encounter with him? Will you humble yourself before him and call out for help? Will you look into the face of Jesus to behold the tender compassion of love as his eyes rest upon you? Will you come so close to him that you may feel his touch? Come and hear the loving voice of the Saviour.

This man deeply touched the sympathies of Jesus. The incident shows Jesus acting in character. The direct appeal of the leper's question cut a passage to the heart of Christ because it petitioned his true nature. That nature has not changed. 'Jesus Christ is the same yesterday and today and forever' (Hebrews 13:8). He is sympathetic to our situation, 'For we do not have a high priest who is unable to sympathize with our weaknesses' (Hebrews 4:15). Do we really understand the loving heart of Jesus? Is this the picture we have of Christ? Do we have problems or needs? In human relationships we sometimes share a problem knowing that the listener does not have the power to change anything. Nevertheless we value their sympathy. But Jesus has both the sympathy and the power if only we will believe!

We are made in the image of God and our capacity for love (frail and flawed as it is) is merely a faint trace of that residual image. What is imperfect in us is perfect in God. In this miracle we get a glimpse of that loving nature and it warms our hearts to him.

An invitation to love

Let us return for a moment to this leper. Imagine how night after night he lay down burdened with disease and without hope. Think of what it was like morning after morning to wake to the realisation of his misery. Are you living a burdened life? Jesus said, 'Come to me, all you who are weary and burdened, and I will give you rest' (Matthew 11:28). Here is where love begins, with the compassion of Christ's touch in our lives! It is very unlikely that your problem is leprosy but perhaps you are emotionally afflicted with depression, anxiety or stress. Or maybe you have never come to Christ to be released from the disease of sin that afflicts every life. Come and cast yourself upon him and he will graciously pardon. He can sympathise because he knows what it is like to be afflicted. In the Garden of Gethsemane Jesus was deeply distressed and troubled, 'My soul is overwhelmed with sorrow to the point of death' (Mark 14:34).

This poor man must have felt miserable. He had to contend with the corroding influence of leprosy as it ate into his flesh. Perhaps you have seen cancer debilitate a loved one? Were you moved to compassion? Of course you were! But that compassion is only a diluted attribute of what is undiluted in Christ. Sometimes all that we can bring to Jesus is our need. This man was a leper and he is so associated with the disease that he is nameless. That is what he is and that is who he is. In our society we tend to identify people by their professions (doctors, teachers etc.). That practice was familiar at the time of Christ. Jesus himself was known as a carpenter: 'Isn't this the carpenter?' (Mark 6:3). It must have been devastating to be cast aside, not only to be redundant but also to take on the identity of an outcast. He couldn't shake off the affliction or the consciousness of it. It pervaded the physical and the psychological. He was a leper; that was his identity.

Have you ever been conscious of your true identity before God? Have you come to that point in your life where you can say with David, 'For I know my transgressions, and my sin is always before me' (Psalm 51:3). It must have been emotionally painful for the leper to present himself to Jesus. As he came within close proximity to the crowd that always attended the Master would he have seen disapproval and disgust registering on the faces of others? What a marked contrast when he beheld the face of Jesus! It was different in the company of fellow lepers. But even there he always saw others as a loathsome reflection of what he was himself.

We must come with our sins in our woeful condition or we cannot come at all. This man begged Jesus on his knees. Have you ever been driven to your knees in this way? Those who are conscious of their unclean condition before a holy God may cast themselves on the compassion of Christ and hear those liberating and loving words, 'Be clean!' We must realise that we cannot help ourselves and overcome our condition. This man's life was radically transformed. In this story we see the power, the love and the will of God working in harmony. May we have that approach of deep faith in our ongoing relationship with God! It is the word and touch of the Master that makes the difference. In all of this we see that defining and describing love is only the first step on a journey that demonstrates love in compassionate action.

The divine disposition

It is important for us in considering love as fruit of the Spirit to come to a better understanding of God's perfect love because it is this love which will manifest itself, to some degree in the life of the believer. Love is the most profound expression of the personality. Therefore, when we talk of love as fruit of the Spirit we are saying that something of the divine disposition ought to come through in our lives. In Christ love becomes a compelling force that drives us to perform loving deeds.

God loves all that he has created whether animal, mineral or vegetable. He loves the physical universe, the ecology he has entrusted to our care and management, animal and vegetable life and the mineral substance of the cosmos. However, God has a special affection for mankind. Humans are the special objects of his love. The personal nature of his love is revealed in his covenant relationship with his people. It is stronger than that of a mother for her children. Thus we read in Isaiah, 'Can a mother forget the baby at her breast and have no compassion on the child she has borne? Though she may forget, I will not forget you' (49:15). Surely in Christ we see the reality of what is said in the next verse in Isaiah, 'See, I have engraved you on the palms of my hands' (v. 16).

The relationship between the prophet Hosea and his harlot wife Gomer illustrates the reality of a love that is based on more than the legality of the covenant. The fidelity of that love is depicted there for us in a way that tells us that God's love is enduring and persevering and willing to suffer. God's love is an expression of his divine identity and in spite of disobedience he continues to love. Hosea, in a sense, is an Old Testament illustration of the New Testament statement 'God is love' (1 John 4:8:16).

God always takes the initiative in love, 'We love because he first loved us' (1 John 4:19). There is nothing of intrinsic value in us that elicits love from God rather his love comes from his nature and is an expression of that attribute (love) which is his very essence. We have the objective truth of his Word that tells us of his love for us and we also have the subjective witness of the Holy Spirit in our hearts to confirm that love.

Love for God

Augustus H. Strong said, 'Love to God is the essence of all virtue'. With regard to the fruit of the Spirit we can say with certainty that love for God will inevitably produce all the other graces listed as fruit of the Spirit. It is out of love that 'joy, peace, patience, kindness, goodness, faithfulness, gentleness and self-control' emerge. One of the first evidences of the fruit of the Spirit is love for God. That initial intensity of love when we first come to know Christ as Saviour, Lord and friend should grow more fervent day by day. Sadly we sometimes see that first love grow colder as time goes by, but that is not as it should be. How natural it should be for the believer to love God.

When Jesus was confronted by the Pharisees and Sadducees to identify the greatest commandment he summed up the essence of the law in his response. Thus we read: 'Hearing that Jesus had silenced the Sadducees, the Pharisees got together. One of them, an expert in the law, tested him with this question: "Teacher, which is the greatest commandment in the Law?" Jesus replied: "Love the Lord your God with all your heart and with all your soul and with all your mind. This is the first and greatest commandment. And the second is like it: Love your neighbour as yourself. All the Law and the Prophets hang on these two commandments" (Matthew 22:34–40).

Leaving aside the second greatest commandment for the moment we must admit that this is a very challenging statement from Christ, which calls on those who profess faith in him to be passionately and wholeheartedly devoted, emotionally, intellectually and spiritually to God. Vance Havner has said, 'The church has no greater need today than to fall in love with Jesus all over again'. These are challenging words that call us to rekindle our passion for Christ and the cause of the kingdom.

There are many evidences in society that people who claim to be Christian are Christian in name only and not in fact Christians at all. This kind of nominal 'Christianity' demonstrates that they do not love God. We hear the precious name of Jesus used in vain and this profanity is thought to be little more than merely a bad social habit, if even that! There is a lack of appreciation for the blessings that God bestows. We see lives given to the works of the flesh and living in flagrant violation of God's laws. But there is a change when conversion takes place and a new awareness of God's love floods into the heart of the believer. There is an awakening of understanding that leads us to appreciate his blessings and to love his name. In considering the statement that 'The fruit of the Spirit is love' we are first and foremost called to manifest that love for God! Why do we love him? We love God because we come to understand and experience his love for us. As Scripture puts it, "We love him because he first loved us" (1 John 4:19). It was he who took the initiative when we were far off and beckoned and drew us in to that great love.

Love seeks love

That marvellous statement by Jesus in John's gospel, 'For God so loved the world that he gave his one and only Son, that whoever believes in him shall not perish but have eternal life' (3:16) tells us of the quality of that love. 'For God *so* loved the world …' In that little word 'so' our attention is drawn to the depth of that great love and the very nature of it. At Calvary we see in that battered and bruised figure upon the cross the form of one despised and rejected, mocked, ridiculed, falsely accused, falsely tried, stripped, whipped and utterly humiliated.

All this was volitional on his part. It was not that things got out of control and went terribly wrong and ended in disaster. Scripture tells us that 'Christ Jesus came into the world to save sinners' (1 Tim.1:15). This was the purpose of his life; his ministry was always directed toward that rescue mission. Why? Because he loved us! If we love him now it is because we have come to realise that.

An awareness and appreciation of God's love makes demands upon us, as love always will. Love calls for a response, not reciprocation, but love seeks love. The quality of God's unconditional love is perfect and the Holy Spirit, active in the life of the believer, seeks to instil and elicit love for God. When this grows to maturity it is the beginning of the fruit of the Spirit.

God is not pleased with mere observance of religious duty; rather he desires and demands a relationship of devoted love. As A. W. Pink said, 'The severest self-denials and the most lavish gifts are of no value in God's esteem unless they are prompted by love'. That love is enjoyed in communion with God and expressed in lives of obedience to him and service for him. It is entirely right that we should have intense feelings for God but our love must be more than that.

God's love is constant but sadly a believer's love for God may cool. If our hearts are blighted with selfishness and sin, that growth in the fruit of 'love' which God desires will be stunted. Let us recall the words of Jesus to the church in Ephesus: 'I know your deeds, your hard work and your perseverance. I know that you cannot tolerate wicked men, that you have tested those who claim to be apostles but are not, and have found them false. You have persevered and have endured hardships for my name, and have not grown weary. Yet I hold this against you: You have forsaken your first love. Remember the height from which you have fallen! Repent and do the things you did at first' (Revelation 2:2–5). In the light of such words the believer is called to check the temperature of his love. The church in Ephesus had not moved away from love but from 'first love'. What is 'first love' if it is not passionate, intense, preoccupying and all consuming! The church at Ephesus is commended for much but the Lord was offended by their cooling love. May we never lose that sense of awe and wonder as expressed by John, 'How great is the love the Father has lavished on us, that we should be called children of God!' (1 John 3:1).

When we consider that God has set his affection on us, that we are chosen by inscrutable divine selection, it should inspire us to worship him and stimulate holiness in living for his glory. May the lover of our souls never have cause to be offended by a love that is professed and not practised passionately! May God through the Holy Spirit cause that fruit of love to grow and ripen in our lives!

Love in the family

The family is a place where traits of character are developed. We must ask ourselves, are we good models of love in our marriages as we live our lives in close proximity to our children? Do we show love to our spouses and children by kindness and patience? Are we courteous and considerate in word and deed to our loved ones? This is the litmus test of love. We live in a world where so many marriages end in divorce and the church of Christ is not immune to the reality of this within its membership. In his book, *The Fruit of the Spirit,* Ron Hembree discusses the necessity for love in marriage. He points out that even in marriages that do not end in divorce there may still be a failure in love! He describes these kinds of marriages as a state of 'undivorced'. He says, 'Love and communication are gone, but the couple remains together because of social pressures, children, finances or some other reason. Tragically the home degenerates into a battlefield of individual rights, sometimes noisy, sometimes silent, but always tense.'[1]

Love for the family of God

Christian love is not necessarily a spontaneous overflow of feeling; rather it is a conscious effort of the will. We can choose to love people we don't like and in doing this we will grow to feel loving toward that person. Mutual love amongst the brethren is what God desires. Matthew Henry said, 'To have the heart glow with mutual love is vastly better than to glare with the most pompous titles, offices or powers'. God desires that love should characterise our relationships. The Christian is born into God's family by faith in Christ and has a whole company of brothers and sisters in the local and universal church. Just as he has a unique new relationship with God he also has a unique new relationship with his fellow believers. His love for God is a vital sign of that new life and his love for fellow believers is also proof that new life exists. Jesus commanded any that would wish to be his disciples to love one another. 'A new command I give you: Love one another. As I have loved you, so you must love one another. By this all men will know that you are my disciples, if you love one another' (John 13:34–35). It may seem strange that Christ should command his disciples to love one another but when we consider the lack of love that exists in human families and sometimes in the family of God we soon realise the necessity of such a command. Nevertheless, being commanded to love may seem like Miss Havisham in Charles Dicken's *Great Expectations* commanding the little boy Pip to play! It seems unnatural to engage in play at the command of another.

We have stated that Christian love need not necessarily be a spontaneous overflow of feeling and we have suggested that it is legitimate to think of it in terms of a conscious effort of the will. However, we might also legitimately say that play ought to be a spontaneous activity that just happens when the moment is right. There is no contradiction here as we shall see. Play may happen very naturally or it may be organised. I might, for example, say to my children stop squabbling and play *Scrabble*! They may object and I may insist and eventually they will get into the spirit of it and soon they will be laughing, until they start squabbling again! But the outcome of obedience to a command to play is fun, and so too the result of obedience to Christ's command to love one another is that we enter into love. Behaving in a loving way can actually produce love in both the recipients and the benefactor. The Lord bestows a blessing on loving attitudes and actions. The love to which we are called is to be a practical outworking of that special affection. As J. R. Lowell put it, 'Every man feels instinctively that all the beautiful sentiments in the world weigh less than a single lovely action'.

In the spiritual realm we are commanded to love one another precisely because we have a propensity not to love one another. We are prone to squabble! When our idea of love falls short of the example cited in 1 Corinthians 13 we become confused about what love is and what it ought to be. Many people in the world and sadly some people in the Christian church think that love *must* be understood as a spontaneous overflow of feeling. Although we are not seeking to deny this aspect of love we suggest a broader understanding. Many people think that when feelings are feeble, love is dying and so they seek that intensity again and again in new relationships. Of course there should be passion in love but we need to think of love as much more than sentimental feeling. As the passage in 1 Corinthians has shown, love 'always perseveres' (v. 7).

Determined effort

Loving the people of God may take a determined effort on our part and we should realise that the Holy Spirit seeks to produce that sense of commitment amongst us. This is the fruit of the Spirit called 'love' and it is evidence of our professed identity as Christians: 'We know that we have passed from death to life, because we love our brothers. Anyone who does not love remains in death. Anyone who hates his brother is a murderer, and you know that no murderer has eternal life in him' (1 John 3:14–15). Just as the apple identifies the tree as an apple tree so too 'love' identifies the believer's true nature and eternal status. The Galatians were suffering from a lack of love, as some churches do, so Paul wrote to them, 'If you keep on biting and devouring each other, watch out or you will be destroyed by each other' (Galatians 5:15). They had once loved one another but they had become legalistic. Love and legalism don't inhabit the same space. Either legalism will drive love away or love will triumph and destroy legalism. This battle between love and legalism had been in progress when Paul wrote to them about life in the Spirit and he longed to see them bearing the fruit of love again.

If Christ died for those who make up the church surely this demands that we love every member of the family of God. Thus we are called to the most magnificent form of love (*agape*), which sees something immensely valuable in its objects. Are we fond of the family of God? Do we cherish the church for which Christ died? How much affection is in our activity? D. L. Moody said, 'A man may be a good doctor without loving his patients; a good lawyer without loving his clients; a good geologist without loving science; but he cannot be a good Christian without love'. The love which the Spirit produces is unconquerable and self-giving, and this should be reflected in our relationships with those within the household of faith. It is a love that ought to be expressed in service to others. Love is the hallmark of the believer. In fact love is like the very signature of God on his work of redemption in us. In seeking to define and describe this love we come to its central importance and we begin to get some measure of its value. It is easy to love those who are like-minded, but true love is shown in the family of God where there are differences. As A. W. Pink put it, 'Love for the brethren is far more than an agreeable society whose views are the same'.

Love should cause us to be concerned for the reputation of the church because the local church is the embassy of God. That God is love! May our hearts be filled with love and stirred to pray for the church in the words we find in Joel: 'Let the priests, who minister before the LORD, weep between the temple porch and the altar. Let them say, "Spare your people, O LORD. Do not make your inheritance an object of scorn, a byword among the nations. Why should they say among the peoples, 'Where is their God?'"' (2:17).

Love for the Lost

We have already considered the first part of Christ's answer to the Pharisees and Sadducees when he summed up the central tenet of the law, and we said then that we would leave aside the second part for the moment. We now pick up where we left off with the words of Christ, 'Love the Lord your God with all your heart and with all your soul and with all your mind. This is the first and greatest commandment. And the second is like it: Love your neighbour as yourself' (Matthew 22:37–39). What does it mean to 'Love your neighbour as yourself'? Our neighbours are those around us in our communities, counties, country and neighbouring countries. In this world of easy access to travel and communication we can truly say that the world has become a global village and that people in what were once far-away places are now our neighbours. So we are instructed to love everybody, whatever their religion or race. We are to bear fruit of this love in our lives. Our love is not to be limited in scope to those who are nearest to us in geographical terms. God leaves us in no doubt about this when he commands us to love our enemies and persecutors, 'I tell you: Love your enemies and pray for those who persecute you' (Matthew 5:44). Francis Schaeffer said, 'All men are our neighbours, and we are to love them as ourselves. We are to do this on the basis of creation, even if they are not redeemed, for all men have value because they are made in the image of God. Therefore they are to be loved even at great cost'. This is a demand that requires supernatural grace. Christ points out the inadequacy of loving only those who reciprocate that love. 'If you love those who love you, what reward will you get? Are not even the tax collectors doing that?' (Matthew 5:46). Only the work of the Holy Spirit in the heart can produce love of this nature and scope.

Just a few verses before he begins to list the fruit of the Spirit Paul says, 'The entire law is summed up in a single command: "Love your neighbour as yourself"' (Galatians 5:14). The law divulges God's intended way of life for mankind. The law deals with every area of life, spiritual, social and personal. The law of God ought to shape our attitudes and stimulate our activity. It is in the law of God that we learn what he expects of our relationships with him and with each other. The law of God leaves us in no doubt about our responsibilities. Paul, like Jesus, says that the word that sums up the law is 'love'. However, we notice that Paul, unlike Jesus, does not refer to love for God as the first principle and essence of the law. Is he saying something different to Christ? We think not. As Paul is writing to a church, that is a group of individuals who have been redeemed and gather in the name of Christ, he assumes that they understand their obligation to love God. However, he is addressing their need to understand and apply the second tenet of the law to 'Love your neighbour as yourself'. The Greek word for 'summed up' has two meanings. It can, obviously, mean *summarised* but it may also mean *fulfilled* as it does in Romans 13:8 'for he who loves his fellow-man has fulfilled the law.' In Galatians, therefore, Paul is saying that it is within the context of new life in Christ that love is made possible within the Christian church and thus it is through the Holy Spirit that the law finds fulfilment.

The Lord's love

Love for others is yet another outward sign of the indwelling Spirit. In this regard the Holy Spirit's presence causes us to be like Jesus. Consider the Lord and his love for sinners. He came to pursue and redeem the lost. He stated this clearly in his ministry when he said 'For the Son of Man came to seek and to save what was lost' (Luke 19:10). His identification with transgressors was such that he was criticised for loving sinners. Thus we read: 'Now the tax collectors and "sinners" were all gathering around to hear him. But the Pharisees and the teachers of the law muttered, "This man welcomes sinners and eats with them"' (Luke.15:1–2). His death for sinners proved his love, 'But God demonstrates his own love for us in this: While we were still sinners, Christ died for us' (Romans 5:8). Spirit-filled people love sinners and minister to them. Christ's love was selfless and sacrificial and it sets for us the standard of love to which we must aspire. Christ himself in his life and death is the supreme example of love, 'Greater love has no-one than this, that he lay down his life for his friends' (John 15:13).

Martin Luther King talked about the regrettable situation that '… Christians … are thermometers that record or register the temperature of majority opinion, not thermostats that transform and regulate the temperature of society.'[2] If we apply this to love it is equally regrettable that we spend so much time bemoaning the absence of love whereas we should be a people who influence others through the love of God which has been shed abroad in our hearts. In a world where there is so much anger, hate and rage we might be inclined to adopt similar attitudes and actions, and that is merely to reflect what society is like. When we respond with love and go out of our way to be proactive in love we influence this world, and that is one of our Christian duties. Love is a conscious effort of the will. It is not sufficient that we can define it or describe it, we must demonstrate it. Sympathising with another person's difficulties and distress is the first step in love. Desiring to help is the second step. Love goes further, love takes that third step and acts compassionately! We do not have to feel loving to act lovingly. This is how we can love our enemies. As we act lovingly our feelings will be transformed too. Feelings follow action and we should not wait to have overwhelming spontaneous feelings before acting. Our love may be spurned, but in loving we are fulfilling our obligations to the Lord even if we never see productive results. Our love can make a difference enriching the church and bringing hope to a lost world. Let us continually bear in mind that everybody needs the love of forgiveness and acceptance. A love that is forgiving is a love that is compelling. A resilient love is not easily bent out of shape. God's love is the kind expressed by Stephen, the first Christian martyr, who cried out as he fell to his knees dying from the blows of stones that battered him 'Lord, do not hold this sin against them' (Acts 7:60). It is a magnificent cry of love that honours and echoes his master's heart who prayed at the moment of his death 'Father, forgive them, for they do not know what they are doing' (Luke 23:34). May that same sentiment reverberate in our hearts and strike the Christian keynote of compassionate love in a world that is out of tune with God! We can harbour resentments against those who hurt us and bear grudges to the grave and in so doing display bitterness. Or we can choose to live out love in a world that desperately needs to experience the authentic love of the Almighty.

A compassionate church

What does the world see when it looks at the church? Does it see a church that is constantly complaining or does it see a church that is compassionate? There is much in this world that concerns us and a confused world is watching us. Do they see a belligerent people brandishing Bibles or do they see a compassionate and caring people that courageously bring a biblical perspective to bear? The world knows the difference between concern and condemnation. We must not be afraid to condemn but always with compassion remembering that Christ cried for a city's impending judgement!

So when we say that 'the fruit of the Spirit is love' we are saying that the Holy Spirit produces in the believer a love for God, a love for the family of God and a love for the lost. We recognise love for God, love for the family of God and love for the lost when we encounter it. May we be people who bear such fruit for God!

Love is not only one of God's attributes; it is an essential part of his nature. Jesus is the personification of perfect love. Love is known essentially by the actions it prompts and Calvary is, therefore, the greatest act of love in the history of humanity! Human love fails but divine love, produced in the believer by the Holy Spirit, flourishes.

Love as fruit of the Spirit in the life of the believer, therefore, is not just sentimental feeling. Rather it is a pragmatic love, which ought to be applied where it is needed. This is perfectly illustrated by Jesus in the story of the Good Samaritan. Christ also expressed an expectation for us to love our fellow Christians when he said: 'My command is this: Love each other as I have loved you' (John 15:12). The Christian cannot be destitute of love for others rather it is the mark of the true believer.

Love for those outside the household of faith is best expressed in evangelistic endeavour to see people reached with the gospel and brought to a place where they become beneficiaries of that great love. Love as fruit of the Spirit is also expressed in the patient endurance of persecution. This point is made in Peter's first epistle: 'But how is it to your credit if you receive a beating for doing wrong and endure it? But if you suffer for doing good and you endure it, this is commendable before God. To this you were called, because Christ suffered for you, leaving you an example, that you should follow in his steps' (1 Peter 2:20–21). Christ is the example *par excellence* of love. Although the believer can never emulate that love he is nonetheless called to imitate it. It is the pattern to follow: 'live a life of love, just as Christ loved us and gave himself up for us as a fragrant offering and sacrifice to God' (Ephesians 5:2). The believer is called to a love of his fellow Christian that emerges from an appreciation that the Christian is one for whom Christ died (Romans 14:15). The existence of this love produces a unity amongst believers (Ephesians 4:2) that becomes a sign to the outside world of the reality of Christian discipleship. Thus Christ said, 'By this all men will know that you are my disciples, if you love one another'

(John 13:35). Our prayer should be that, by God's grace, we might bear the fruit of the Spirit, beginning with love.

Jesus looked beyond people's external circumstances and status and saw their need. His love is perfectly demonstrated in his willingness to forgive. It is obvious that if we are to live this kind of love we must be linked to the supernatural source of that great love. We can only be connected to God through the blood of Jesus and it is in this connection that love can be learned and lived.

Notes on Chapter 1

1 **Ron Hembree,** *The Fruit of the Spirit* (Baker Books, 1969, reprinted 1996, Spire),
2 **Martin Luther King,** *Strength to Love* (Collins Fount Paperback, 1977), p.19

Chapter 2

Joy

'But the fruit of the Spirit is ... joy ...'

Friedrich Nietzsche summarised his critique of the Christians of his time in the words of Zarathushtra (Zoroaster): 'They would have to sing better songs to me that I might believe in their Redeemer: his disciples would have to look more redeemed!' This criticism has a sting because we recognise some truth in it. Joy ought to be an essential characteristic of the Christian! A joyless Christian appears to be a contradiction to the truth of redemption. Consider the words of Psalm 126:

When the LORD brought back the captives to Zion, we were like men who dreamed. Our mouths were filled with laughter, our tongues with songs of joy. Then it was said among the nations, 'The LORD has done great things for them.' The LORD has done great things for us, and we are filled with joy. Restore our fortunes, O LORD, like streams in the Negev. Those who sow in tears will reap with songs of joy. He who goes out weeping, carrying seed to sow, will return with songs of joy, carrying sheaves with him.

In this psalm we are given a picture of joy and we learn something of its nature, intensity and expression. The cause of the joy to which the psalmist refers is the fact that those who were in exile are now restored to Zion. Their hearts are filled with the pleasure that their new status presents. There is gladness in their spirits induced by contemplating the wonderful works of God in their lives. They have been freed from foreign oppression and a dominion where they were slaves under cruel taskmasters. It is this thought that causes joy to fill their hearts. Surely the contemplation of our redemption from the empire of darkness and the new opportunities that our freedom affords produces a deep satisfaction within our hearts. The Lord is credited with their restoration and is therefore the source of their joy.

This psalm begins with an acknowledgement that it is God who has done something marvellous for them and it is thrilling to contemplate. This was like a dream come true. God had fulfilled the desire of their hearts and they laughed and sang because they had something to rejoice in and something to sing about. There is nothing superficial or half-hearted in their appreciation of what God has achieved for them. The psalm says their 'mouths were *filled* with laughter'. The sense conveyed in this is that they were overwhelmed with such a deep sense of joy that it overflowed in laughter.

The true nature of joy

Now the Holy Spirit desires to produce such fruit in the believer today by the same means. It is in considering the wonderful redemptive work of Christ that the believer is stimulated to appreciate his new status in Jesus. This in turn causes the Christian to enter into a joy that is rooted in salvation and nourished in relationship with God. Thus the Christian comes to an understanding of the true nature of joy. Infused with such a sense of joy which cannot be contained the believer is characteristically happy and celebrates his delight in exultant songs of praise to his God.

It is very interesting to observe the stated outcome of their rapture. The psalm says, 'Then it was said among the nations, "The LORD has done great things for them"'. The result of their evident joy was that others, outside covenant relationship with God, noticed their gladness. This was a joy that was observable. It was not whispered in secret but sung with cheerfulness so that the surrounding communities also came to bear testimony that "The LORD has done great things for them". What an amazing outcome! The application for us today is obvious. If we are a people characterised by joy and our lives are lived as a celebration of redemption then others will take notice. Moreover they may be brought to acknowledge that the source of our joy and the cause of our satisfaction are related to what God has done for us in Christ! The psalm says that they were *'filled* with joy' and we do well to notice the intensity of that consciousness. We can never enter into such depth of feeling unless and until we appreciate the true value of what God has done for us in redemption.

Yet in this psalm there is recognition that there may be more blessing sought and secured from the hand of God. Thus the prayer of their hearts is expressed in the words 'Restore our fortunes'. These exiles had returned to Zion and they realised that although the return was thrilling to contemplate, it was nevertheless only the beginning of potential blessing. Restoration begins with reconciliation and our God is pleased to '… restore … the years that the locust hath eaten' (Joel 2:25 AV).

There is also in this psalm an acknowledgement that sorrow often precedes joy and that sorrow too may be the experience of those who labour for God. Somebody has said, 'joys are our wings; sorrows are our spurs'. It is not possible to be joyous all the time in this world of sin. Jesus wept at the grave of his friend Lazarus and wailed over the rebelliousness of the inhabitants of Jerusalem. We are human and experience a range of emotions including sorrow. That is a normal part of life and it is an unrealistic expectation to think that the Christian ought always to be joyous. That can only, ultimately, lead to frustration, disappointment and even disillusionment. We ought to be careful on this point and not to create the impression within our churches that it is somehow wrong to be unhappy. A Christian may be unhappy because of particular circumstances in their lives which cause them great heartache. A Christian may suffer from depression and because of a chemical imbalance in the brain they do not produce enough of the happy hormones to stimulate cheerfulness. This, however, should be the exception to the rule. Even in such circumstances when a Christian is not cheerful he may still be content in Christ.

Jesus wept

It will be instructive for us to consider the question 'why did Jesus weep at the grave of Lazarus?' In John 11 Mary, the one who showed her love for Jesus by pouring perfume on his feet and wiping them with her hair, says to Jesus 'Lord, the one you love is sick' (v. 3). Jesus loved Martha, her sister and Lazarus and others observed this: 'Then the Jews said, "See how he loved him!"' (v. 36). Jesus responded with the words, 'This sickness will not end in death' (v. 4). Death is not the end. This life is not all that there is! If Jesus knew what the outcome would be, why did he weep at the grave of Lazarus when he knew he was going to raise Lazarus from the dead? In the narrative itself, however, we notice that it is when Mary arrives, broken-hearted and in tears (and others too are weeping) that Jesus wept. He could hardly bear to look at Mary, mourning and crushed with sorrow without being moved to deep emotion. His feeling is described with three distinct words. The first of these is 'deeply moved' which is an expression of anger. Perhaps Jesus was expressing his resentment against the ravages of death that had entered the human world because of sin. Sin is the underlying cause of all suffering and sorrow. The second word expresses agitation, showing that Jesus was not indifferent to the prevailing mood of sorrow. Lazarus had been a friend and Jesus shared in the common feeling of grief over his death. Overcome by emotion he spontaneously burst into tears. His tears were an expression of love, not only for Lazarus but also for Mary, Martha and others. They were tears of genuine sympathy. As the writer to the Hebrews says: 'For we do not have a high priest who is unable to sympathise …' (Hebrews 4:15). Jesus is not just a compassionate witness to our suffering. He is all that but more. He is a fellow sufferer. His heart is crushed with the sorrow of sin. Isaiah speaks prophetically of Jesus as 'a man of sorrows' and as one who was 'familiar with suffering'.

God instructs us to 'Rejoice with those who rejoice; mourn with those who mourn' (Romans 12:15). Did you ever cry at the funeral of a believer? Did your tears mean that you don't believe in the resurrection of the dead? Of course not! We cry at these times because God has made us, in his image, people with deep affections for others. We are created beings in body, mind and spirit. When the body is nourished and rested and the mind is stimulated, content and calm we can be relatively happy. But true joy is found when our spirits are in harmony with God. That is why Christian people who have been deprived of liberty, food and shelter can still say that they have joy. Although our joy may be enhanced by these basic necessities it does not depend on them. Our joy is in Jesus.

A time for rejoicing

Ecclesiastes tells us there is, 'a time to weep and a time to laugh' (3:4). In other words there are appropriate occasions for regrets and for rejoicing. There are times for crying and times for celebrating. As we have already noted Paul says, 'Rejoice with those who rejoice; mourn with those who mourn' (Romans 12:15). Jesus said, 'Blessed are you who weep now, for you will laugh' (Luke 6:21) and 'Woe to you who laugh now, for you will mourn and weep' (Luke 6:25). In other words Jesus is saying if you weep over your sins now and that sorrow turns your heart to God, you will be comforted and know joy in the future. On the other hand if you continue to frolic in your folly and sinfulness and refuse to repent you will know future sorrow. These words of Christ indicate that those who pursue laughter as an end in itself and indulge in godless pursuits to fulfil that objective will regret it throughout eternity. But he also promises laughter as a future blessing to those who are remorseful and repentant. One of Job's 'comforters', Bildad, says: 'He will yet fill your mouth with laughter and your lips with shouts of joy' (Job 8:21). That, however, in context, is a superficial statement that is little more than a pious platitude. Solomon says, 'Laughter ... is foolish ...' (Ecclesiastes 2:2) and 'Sorrow is better than laughter ...' (Ecclesiastes 7:3). His serious view of life shows contempt for superficiality and frivolity as the following verse shows: 'Like the crackling of thorns under the pot, so is the laughter of fools' (Ecclesiastes 7:6). In James we read, 'Grieve, mourn and wail. Change your laughter to mourning and your joy to gloom' (4:9). Are we to suppose that this attitude is to characterise the Christian life? I think not. James was appealing for evident repentance to a hedonistic people. I do not think we are meant to put on dour masks throughout life, especially while singing 'O Happy Day'![1]

Misplaced merriment

We learn from this brief sketch that the preponderance of Scripture cautions against misplaced merriment. For example, Solomon's pursuit of pleasure was essentially hedonistic and the laughter derived from such a lifestyle is denounced as superficial and sinful. He learned that being preoccupied with the temporal world of thrills and the pursuit of happiness through possessions could only produce disappointment. The seriousness of man's lost condition is central to forming an appropriate mood. The conviction of the Holy Spirit must bring about contrition and confession of sin and sinfulness. Paul says, 'Godly sorrow brings repentance that leads to salvation' (2 Corinthians 7:10).

We have looked closely at the psalm that remembers past blessings where the psalmist says 'Our mouths were filled with laughter, our tongues with songs of joy' (Psalm 126:2). But we could add that there is a connection between laughter and joy inasmuch as laughter may be an audible expression of joy. Peter refers to believers as those who 'believe in him and are filled with an inexpressible and glorious joy' (1 Peter 1:8). In this sense laughter can never fully give expression to real joy.

Laughter may or may not be an expression of joy. Consider these words, 'Even in laughter the heart may ache' (Proverbs 14:13). It seems that laughter may be employed to evade the conviction of the Holy Spirit. The following words seem particularly apt, 'I make myself laugh at everything, for fear of having to weep'.[2] Nevertheless as somebody once said 'a cheerful countenance has a lot of face value'!

Authentic joy

God desires to be glorified in our lives and this work is begun in redemption. We are to be diligent in seeking to cultivate Christian character so that God may be honoured. God wants a representative community of people whose lives are transformed and joyous. He desires to develop disciples who model the message of God's grace and thereby glorify him. Joy, as fruit of the Spirit, will bring glory to God. People see through emotions that are artificial or superficial but authentic joy bears testimony to his work in our lives. God wants to do a deep work in our lives and under the supreme authority of the Holy Spirit develop character that is marked with joy. We are not to be flippant people because inappropriate levity is incongruous with the solemn nature of our message. Real joy is not frivolous or facetious. Rather it is a gladness that overflows from real satisfaction and deep contentment. This can only be fully known in Christ. Some of us are more temperamentally suited to joy than others, but the Holy Spirit desires to produce joy in all believers. This joy is not necessarily about expressing humour (although it might be) but it is about rejoicing in what Christ has done for us in redemption and being genuinely and obviously glad to belong to him. I do not believe that the ministry of Christ was entirely without humour. For example, I think Christ was being humorous when he said, 'You blind guides! You strain out a gnat but swallow a camel' (Matthew 23:24), and I would imagine that it made people laugh.

Joy ought to be a spontaneous result of being filled with the Holy Spirit. We see this as a natural outcome of the Holy Spirit's activity in Acts 13:52, 'And the disciples were filled with joy and with the Holy Spirit'. Joy should be the basic mood of congregational gatherings. It is not necessary that joy be expressed in exuberant jubilation. Joy may be expressed vivaciously or quietly. We don't have to be ecstatic in our public worship to exhibit that joy, but God expects us to be joyous! Our joy is rooted in the recognition that the dominion of evil is already broken through the power of Christ and that death, the devil, and demons no longer possess any claim upon believers. The forces of forgiveness, reconciliation and resurrection are already effective in the believer. The contemplation of this reality effectively arouses and sustains joy in the hearts of those who belong to Christ.

The believer's joy is based on such a solid foundation that even in the midst of the numerous spiritual, physical, psychological and emotional conflicts of life he is capable of regarding all sufferings and afflictions from the perspective of overcoming them, if not now, then in the future. This is the perspective of victory over problems already achieved in Christ. We are not guaranteed protection *from* storms in the Christian life but we are sure of protection *in* those storms. Remember that storms came to both the wise and foolish builders in the parable told by Christ. One built his house on sand while the other built upon a rock. Both experienced storms but the outcome was different for both. The house built on sand did not withstand the force of the wind but the one that had the solid foundation endured. When Paul was shipwrecked (Acts 27) God was with him in the storm. He still had to endure the experience of being shipwrecked but he had the presence and protection of God at all times. Christian joy is established on solid ground and the constant companionship of Christ.

Spirit-produced joy is not something superficial or artificial. It cannot be worked up from within ourselves by ourselves because it is the fruit of the Holy Spirit. Some people seem to think that if they create a certain church ambience and crank up the razzmatazz in the style of worship that it will lead to joy in the lives of believers. This is an utterly superficial and profoundly misguided approach to producing joy in the Christian life. Real joy is more than the kind of emotion that can be artificially stimulated (though frequently well intentioned) in this way. The world craves that hit or buzz. It seeks it in alcohol, sexual promiscuity and the use of 'recreational' drugs. This is the devil's counterfeit. It is the Christian who has authentic joy. It is a joy rooted in and related to the work of Christ in salvation and sanctification.

The Joy of Salvation

The joy of salvation is a very precious thing indeed. Salvation is something to be celebrated and enjoyed. There is a past aspect to our salvation in that our sins have been forgiven and this stimulates joy. There is a present aspect to our salvation in that we have the Holy Spirit to guide, comfort and reassure us, through the illumination of his Word, that we belong to him. Then there is the future aspect of our salvation that one day we are going to be with the Lord. And we anticipate his return with joy!

We are not meant to merely have nostalgic memories of that initial encounter with God. Joy is not just something to be remembered; rather it is to be an invigorating force in the life of the Christian. However, that initial joy of the newborn Christian may be gradually displaced because spiritual warfare between the flesh and the Spirit begins when one is born again. Consequently, one reason for the absence of joy in the lives of believers is the entrance of sin. Somebody once put it like this: 'nothing will stop your song quicker than your sin'. The joy of salvation needs to be nurtured and maintained. If a Christian engages in some act or assumes some attitude that is an offence to God he will find that joy is a delicate fruit that is susceptible to changes in the temperature of the heart. Joy is fed on devotion to God and love for others and any cooling of that love will affect the ripening of joy as fruit of the Spirit.

In the great penitential psalm of David, written after he had committed adultery with Bathsheba and commissioned the murder of her husband Uriah, we read these words, 'Restore to me the joy of your salvation' (Psalm 51:12). He had lost that sense of delight in his relationship with God. He had transgressed in breaking the clear laws of God and in doing what he knew to be wrong he robbed himself of spiritual pleasure. At some point in his life David had come to realise this as we see throughout the Psalms, for example, in the following words: 'The precepts of the LORD are right, giving joy to the heart' (Psalm 19:8). That is one of the terrible things about sin that we do not often take into account, that sin robs us of joy. David desired illicit sexual pleasure and was prepared to do anything in order to gratify that lust. Although he satiated his sexual craving he did so at great personal cost. He was like a child who overindulged his appetite with the dainties arrayed at a party and soon found himself to be sick and regretting his lack of restraint. This is not to trivialise the seriousness of what he had done, rather to show the silliness of it from the point of view of his own spiritual and emotional welfare. The point is that if we allow our spiritual integrity to be compromised we will become ill and the first symptom of that malady of the heart is the withering away of joy.

So David wrote with a burdened heart. He had lost the joy of salvation and longed to have it back again. Once a person comes to know the joy of salvation nothing else will suffice as a substitute. The joy of salvation is the joy of knowing sins forgiven. That is where joy begins. True joy cannot be experienced without this understanding of salvation. Joy is a theme of many psalms as illustrated in this verse, 'You have made known to me the path of life; you will fill me with joy in your presence, with eternal pleasures at your right hand' (Psalm 16:11). Joy flourishes in the presence of God; it derives nourishment from the love *of* God, love *for* God, love for the family of God and love for the lost.

Living a full life

Jesus said, 'I have come that they may have life, and have it to the full' (John 10:10). He desires his disciples to enter into a spiritual life that is qualitatively different to their experience of life before following him. He speaks of this new life as an abundant life. He wants his followers to enjoy life and know bountiful blessing. Thus the Holy Spirit seeks to produce joy in the lives of believers. This is a joy that is meant to be experienced in the here and now. The joy of being a child of God and knowing heaven is ahead anticipates a future hope that influences our perspective. This in turn is reflected in our attitudes and actions and how we live in the here and now in anticipation of that future hope. In this sense it is not a dim and distant desire for joy as a posthumous compensation for the misery we have to endure in this life. Rather joy is a deposit of that eternal hope. It is an advance payment that God expects us to spend extravagantly in this life. As

Thomas Watson put it, 'Here joy begins to enter into us; there, we enter into joy.'

Joy is not meant to be merely a garment displayed on a window; it is designed so that it might be animated on the main street when it is worn. It enhances the appearance of the wearer and wins the admiration of onlookers! We bring glory to God by displaying joy in our lives. Imagine a young woman who becomes engaged to be married; one would naturally expect her to be happy and one would be rather concerned for her if she never displayed that joy! The Christian is betrothed to Christ and the wedding day is approaching. In the meantime we have a dynamic relationship with him. His love is perfect and we are the objects of that love. Surely it is natural for us to radiate evident joy. 'Let us rejoice and be glad and give him glory! For the wedding of the Lamb has come, and his bride has made herself ready' (Revelation 19:7).

Abiding joy

Real joy commences from being at peace with God. 'Therefore, since we have been justified through faith, we have peace with God through our Lord Jesus Christ' (Romans 5:1). Ultimately that joy will be complete when we behold him face to face, but in the interim joy continues through abiding in him. We need to know the joy of a fruitful life in Christ. In a well-known passage of Scripture Jesus speaks of the necessity of abiding in him if we are to be fruitful. Let us look at this wonderful passage:

I am the vine; you are the branches. If a man remains in me and I in him, he will bear much fruit; apart from me you can do nothing. If anyone does not remain in me, he is like a branch that is thrown away and withers; such branches are picked up, thrown into the fire and burned. If you remain in me and my words remain in you, ask whatever you wish, and it will be given you. This is to my Father's glory, that you bear much fruit, showing yourselves to be my disciples. As the Father has loved me, so have I loved you. Now remain in my love. If you obey my commands, you will remain in my love, just as I have obeyed my Father's commands and remain in his love. I have told you this so that my joy may be in you and that your joy may be complete (John 15:5–11).

The key to bearing fruit is abiding in Christ. John knew what that meant, and in the gospel accounts we encounter him leaning on the bosom of Christ. This is the safest and most comfortable place to allow our souls to repose. In any evaluation of our spiritual condition we need to ask: are we abiding in Christ? We need to evaluate our spiritual condition often. One appropriate place for that kind of introspective inventory or spiritual stocktaking is the Lord's Table. That is a time appointed by the Lord for us to examine ourselves. 'A man ought to examine himself before he eats of the bread and drinks of the cup' (1 Corinthians 11:28). Is the joy of the Lord our daily experience? If not, why not? What needs to be corrected? Are we abiding in Christ? Are we drawing daily life from Jesus? Are we bearing fruit for him? Are we fully surrendered to him? Are we wholehearted or half-hearted? Are we hot, cold or lukewarm? Remember love that is tepid in temperature is totally unacceptable to God! Consider the words that he spoke to the church at Ephesus: 'So, because you are lukewarm—neither hot nor cold—I am about to spit you out of my mouth' (Revelation 3:16). Are we keeping a strong devotional life by feeding on God's Word daily and praying fervently and frequently? Are we confessing all known sin and doing everything we can to 'keep the unity of the Spirit through the bond of peace'? (Ephesians 4:3).

We must not be cut off from that vital union with him because to do so is to become barren and impotent. Just as the branch withers and dies if it is cut off from that vital union, so too we shrivel up and become utterly unproductive if we do not abide in him. The Holy Spirit will not produce the fruit of joy on dead and disconnected branches. God expects us to cultivate healthy habits that bear fruit for his glory, and so we should produce joy within our lives and be a source of stimulating that joy in others. We must dwell in Christ. If we are joined in intimate and organic unity to Christ the fruit of joy will be a natural outcome. Separation through sin spoils the potential harvest of that joy. That joy is not just for our benefit or the benefit of others, it is also something that God desires to enjoy! It is a challenging thought that we can be a source of joy to God. Why did Jesus speak to his disciples about being the vine and they (us too) the branches? We need not wonder about this issue because being the perfect teacher he explained that to them! Thus we read in John 15:11, 'I have told you this so that my joy may be in you and that your joy may be complete'.

Evangelistic joy

The apostle Paul spoke of the believers at Thessalonica as a source of joy to him: 'For what is our hope, our joy, or the crown in which we will glory in the presence of our Lord Jesus Christ when he comes? Is it not you? Indeed, you are our glory and joy' (1 Thessalonians 2:19–20). He revelled in them as a father might take keen delight in his children. This was a church that God graciously started through the ministry of Paul (Acts 16:1–9).

One of the reasons for joy in heaven is the repentance of sinners: 'there is rejoicing in the presence of the angels of God over one sinner who repents' (Luke 15:10). To be instrumental in leading people to faith in Christ is a source of joy in heaven and on earth. Does anything thrill the hearts of the people of God more than seeing somebody come to Jesus in faith and repentance? If we lack joy in our lives maybe we should seek to find it by reaching out to the lost. If God deigns to bless our efforts it will be a tremendous source of joy to ourselves as well as others and, indeed, heaven itself! The joy of deliverance is both wonderful to experience and wonderful to behold. Let us recall the miraculous incident of Acts 3 where Peter is used of God to heal a crippled beggar: 'Then Peter said, "Silver or gold I do not have, but what I have I give you. In the name of Jesus Christ of Nazareth, walk." Taking him by the right hand, he helped him up, and instantly the man's feet and ankles became strong. He jumped to his feet and began to walk. Then he went with them into the temple courts, walking and jumping, and praising God' (vs.6–8). In this account of a physical healing we have a beautiful illustrative picture of what Jesus has done for the helpless and impoverished sinner. The effect ought to be the same. Our spiritual step is quickened with life and the freedom we enter into is a thrill to our hearts. This new surge of energy causes us to bound forward into the presence of God. Just as this man headed for the temple and entered it with a heart full of joy, so too we joyously praise our God for the miracle he has wrought in us. Such exuberant joy cannot be contained and we feel impelled to acknowledge God as the source of our joy and the one who sustains that joy.

Anticipating joy

Joy makes the achievement of our spiritual objectives more attainable. In other words, what we set out to do in the spiritual life is more likely to succeed if we approach it with a confidence in the fact that our labour will lead to joy. That hope of a joyous outcome is what keeps us going. In difficult circumstances it becomes our focus. We know that in obedience and in pleasing God we will be blessed. The anticipation of joy to come made the cross bearable for Jesus and this ought to be a source of encouragement and inspiration to us. As the writer to the Hebrews puts it, 'Let us fix our eyes on Jesus, the author and perfecter of our faith, who for the joy set before him endured the cross, scorning its shame, and sat down at the right hand of the throne of God' (Hebrews 12:2). Christ was focused on the joy that the fulfilment of his ministry's mission would ultimately achieve. In that frame of mind we can follow very difficult paths knowing that he has gone before us. Joy is a light that leads us home. Christian joy is such that it is not subdued by great need. In the words of Habakkuk: 'Though the fig-tree does not bud and there are no grapes on the vines, though the olive crop fails and the fields produce no food, though there are no sheep in the pen and no cattle in the stalls, yet I will rejoice in the LORD, I will be joyful in God my Saviour' (3:17–18).

Whatever the prevailing circumstances might be the believer has a redeemed will that is determined to rejoice and be joyful in his Saviour. This was the attitude of the apostles when they were beaten and commanded to silence. Thus we read in Acts 5:41, 'The apostles left the Sanhedrin, rejoicing because they had been counted worthy of suffering disgrace for the Name.' James exhorted suffering believers to endure persecution with these words, 'Consider it pure joy, my brothers, whenever you face trials of many kinds, because you know that the testing of your faith develops perseverance.' (1:2–3). The Holy Spirit will not ask us to do something without supplying the supernatural grace needed in such circumstances. Thus we may believe that joy is possible in all situations. Let us hold out this hope to those who are grieving and discouraged.

Savouring and sustaining joy

Joy as a fruit of the Spirit comes from the activity of the Holy Spirit in the life of the believer by leading people to faith, wholeness and maturity in Christ. Let us savour the simple joys God sends our way. Let us open our hearts to the ordinary joy of common grace and the special joy of extraordinary grace. There are so many things we take for granted that we can miss the joy they give. We may get so familiar with the beauty of the world all around us and so casual about family, friendship and fellowship that we miss the potential joy they provide.

We are to be careful not to grieve the Holy Spirit (Ephesians 4:30). We are to be careful not to quench the flame that the Holy Spirit kindles in us (1 Thessalonians 5:19). In other words, if we live by the Spirit (Galatians 5:16) then the Spirit will produce that fruit of joy in our lives. Joy is grounded upon God and derived from him. It comes from the harmony of God's heart and our hearts. Oswald Chambers put it like this, 'The joy that Jesus gives is the result of our disposition being at one with his own disposition'. The words of Peter should speak of the condition of all believers, 'Though you have not seen him, you love him; and even though you do not see him now, you believe in him and are filled with an inexpressible and glorious joy' (1 Peter 1:8). There is an ineffable and transcendent quality to that joy of the Spirit that makes it unspeakably exquisite and indescribable. Our prayer is that of Paul for the Roman church, 'May the God of hope fill you with all joy and peace as you trust in him, so that you may overflow with hope by the power of the Holy Spirit' (Romans 15:13). Our joy is connected with our hope in Christ and we can truly say with the psalmist 'in him our hearts rejoice' (Psalm 33:21).

There are special occasions in our lives when we experience joy, but there is no greater occasion for joy than when we encounter the risen Christ, and the Word of God becomes meaningful as it is mediated in our hearts through his Spirit. Let us consider one such occasion in Scripture when two dejected disciples met Jesus (Luke 24:13–32; Mark 16:12–13).

A mosaic of the Master

The story of the two disciples on the road to Emmaus and their encounter with Jesus is a precious gem in the gospels of Mark and Luke. Here we meet two disciples returning home from a funeral. Jesus approached them but they did not recognise him. They must have experienced all sorts of emotions. Their hopes had been crushed and they must have felt remorseful, baffled and perplexed. But disappointment turns to bewilderment as they talk about the reports of the empty tomb and the possibility that Jesus is alive. It ought to have been a day of great joy and celebration but they were not walking in the light of the resurrection. Jesus stepped into that gloomy situation.

We know what he was like before his resurrection. He chose to be born in humble circumstances. He is the one who showed such compassion to many who found him approachable. We meet him weeping over the impending judgement of Jerusalem. At the grave of a friend he weeps with those who are mourning. He enters into their sorrow and his soul is disturbed. Jesus was silent at his trial and caring in death. He reached out to the repentant thief with the promise of heaven. He was tough on hypocrisy but tender to the helpless. But what was he like after the resurrection? Had his nature altered? This story shows that he had not changed, 'Jesus Christ is the same yesterday and today and forever' (Hebrews 13:8). Let us view the risen Christ as he interacts with these disciples and see if we learn anything about how he communicates with his people today.

We see that he draws alongside his disciples and walks with them. He is with them on their journey. They do not recognise him at first but he is close to them, listening to them and drawing them out in conversation. The Lord is always close to those who are discouraged: 'The LORD is close to the broken-hearted and saves those who are crushed in spirit' (Psalm 34:18). He ministers to them: 'He heals the broken-hearted and binds up their wounds' (Psalm 147:3). In fact this aspect of his work is clearly identified at the outset of his ministry when he reads from the scroll in the synagogue at Nazareth, '… He has sent me to bind up the broken-hearted …' (Isaiah 61:1b, which Jesus read in Luke 4:18b). The resurrection has not made him remote from his disciples. The triumphant Christ still takes time to dispel doubt and sorrow and tutor his disciples by coming into their situation.

Problems sometimes prevent us from entering into joy. Christ cares for the problems that his people have. Jesus says, 'What are you discussing together as you walk along?' (Luke 24:17). He knew what they were talking about but wanted them to tell him. Just as today! Jesus knows our concerns and the things that occupy our conversations but he desires us to talk to him about them. The problem is they think he is dead! Are we sometimes guilty of going about under a cloud of gloom as if God were dead? He is concerned about the things that trouble us and wants us to talk to him.

Blazing hearts

He set their hearts on fire and he can still do this if we allow him to help us put the resurrection in perspective. They remember a better day and their hearts needed re-kindling: once those hearts blazed with a passionate zeal for his cause. The flames in their hearts had consumed them but now those embers are smouldering under a bed of grey ash! Once they had expected great things from Jesus but now they just discuss him. It is all too easy for us, as disciples of Christ, to allow ourselves to become like them. We too can fail to fully comprehend the significance of the resurrection by not living in the power of that reality.

Scripture stimulates joy

Notice how Jesus set their hearts on fire. He took them to the Scriptures: 'And beginning with Moses and all the Prophets, he explained to them what was said in all the Scriptures concerning himself' (Luke 24:27). What a Bible study that must have been! Christ is the key to the Old Testament. He is there in type and shadow and as the promised Messiah. He is the golden thread woven through the fabric of both Testaments. Bible study can be so profitable if Christ is our tutor! 'Were not our hearts burning within us while he talked with us on the road and opened the Scriptures to us?' (Luke 24:32).

They missed the joy of the resurrection because they failed to pay enough attention to the Word of God. Neglecting the study of God's Word will result in us missing out on so much. In fact it is only when we see how all the Scriptures are centred in Christ that we will be able to fully appreciate them.

Their faith is restored through fellowship with Christ. That is what happened. They met with Jesus, he invited them to tell him the things that troubled them, they disclose those things to him and he listens and teaches them. They have bits of the jigsaw but they cannot put it together. He assembles the pieces for them and it reveals a self-portrait, in mosaic. This is a turning point where their vision and understanding are altered and it is the beginning of a joyous journey. Luke ends his gospel account with the disciples witnessing the ascension of Jesus into heaven and we note his closing words: 'Then they worshiped him and returned to Jerusalem with great joy. And they stayed continually at the temple, praising God.' (Luke 24:52–53). May we never lose that sense of joy in knowing that Jesus is risen and ascended and may that joy draw us together in worship!

New direction

That wonderful encounter with their Lord had the effect of changing their direction, they return to Jerusalem, a seven-mile trip! It was such a vital encounter that it made them seek out a gathering of other disciples 'they found the Eleven and those with them assembled together' (v. 33). I imagine them breathless with joy as they meet the others. He made them a blessing to others and it was while they were sharing in the truth of the resurrection that Jesus came among them. It was true fellowship (not routine) that brought them together in faith and hope in the resurrected Christ. They were excited by the possibilities opened up to them by the resurrection. What a blessing it is to gather together in the light of the reality of the resurrection. What a joy!

That is what is needed today; joyous hearts that are on fire for God. Many in the world are ignorant of the resurrection; many deny it and are hostile to it. Many are indifferent about the resurrection. What about the Christian, how do we live in the light of it? We are certainly not ignorant of it or hostile to it. Perhaps it would be unfair to say that some believers are indifferent to it but maybe some are a bit casual about it. Are we on fire or just lukewarm? We tend to blow hot and cold. We have already noted that Jesus speaking to the church of Laodicea said: 'So, because you are lukewarm—neither hot nor cold—I am about to spit you out of my mouth'. It is a solemn thought to contemplate that God does not like mediocrity! The Christian's critics might have cause to complain that the believer is a cold-hearted hot head. If only they could see warm-hearted, cool-headed confidence in Christ and the unspeakable joy he imparts.

Recognising the resurrected Christ

As they shared a meal together they recognised him, 'When he was at the table with them, he took bread, gave thanks, broke it and began to give it to them. Then their eyes were opened and they recognised him' (vv. 30–31). Perhaps it was the manner in which he gave thanks as he broke the bread that caused them to recognise him. Maybe they were familiar with his pattern of prayer, tone of voice or some gesture. His identity had been concealed from them, now it was revealed. I like to think that maybe it was the scars on his hands that caused them to understand. O may we get a glimpse of those scars that it might lead to a deeper understanding of who he is and what he has done for us! May our hearts be stimulated with joy rooted in the hope of the resurrection and all its promise for today and tomorrow! Let us recapture joy in Jesus as we yield not only to his residency in our lives but to his reigning authority.

Joy in the church of Christ

Joy was a characteristic of the early church. In Acts 8 we read of Philip's ministry at Samaria. He preached Christ and the people heard and heeded the message of the gospel and were freed from demon possession and many were healed of physical disabilities. Then Luke tells us, 'So there was great joy in that city' (v. 8). This is the inevitable outcome of the work of the Holy Spirit. Then later in the same chapter Philip comes upon the Ethiopian eunuch who was reading Isaiah 53. Philip explains the gospel from that Old Testament passage and this Ethiopian treasurer is converted and baptised. Then Luke says the man, 'went on his way rejoicing' (v. 39). Later in Acts 16 we read the dramatic account of the conversion of the Philippian jailer who was suicidal because he thought his prisoners had escaped. But Paul called out to him and when he discovered that Paul and Silas had not absconded he inquired about the way of salvation. They spoke the Word of the Lord to him and all the others in his household with the result that the jailer and his family were converted and baptised. Then Luke tells us 'he was filled with joy because he had come to believe in God—he and his whole family' (v. 34).

Joy was also a feature of Old Testament Hebrew worship. The Jewish community was so renowned for joyous singing that their Babylonian captors taunted them on this issue. Thus we read in Psalm 137, which recounts that time in the history of Israel, 'for there our captors asked us for songs, our tormentors demanded songs of joy; they said, "Sing us one of the songs of Zion!"' (v. 3). Our spirituality is to be enjoyed not endured. As we recall the words of Paul to the Thessalonians surely we remember that what he said of them we can say of ourselves: 'you welcomed the message with the joy given by the Holy Spirit' (1 Thessalonians 1:6). The word used here for joy (*chara*) is the word used in Galatians for joy as fruit of the Spirit; it speaks of joy given by the Spirit. The might of our Maker and Master is at work in the believer to produce this joy. In the words of Nehemiah, 'the joy of the LORD is your strength' (8:10). Joy comes from knowing our sins forgiven, knowing the sufficiency of his sacrifice, knowing our status in Christ and knowing the assurance of heaven is ours in the hereafter.

The right route to joy

Real joy eludes those who do not walk in the Spirit. The world pursues joy through the attainment of wealth, power, status and harmful recreational activity and substances, but many have been disillusioned in failing to find happiness in such pursuits. People change jobs and walk out on marriages in the mistaken belief that happiness is to be found in a salary increase or new relationships only to find themselves as miserable as they were in the past. Money and pleasure is not the key to joy as Solomon found out. If we could heed his wisdom we would spare ourselves so much misery. God is a good father who wants his children to be happy. Jesus said that he desires us to be joyous: 'I have told you this so that my joy may be in you and that your joy may be complete' (John 15:11). Christ's joy came from an eternal rather than earthly perspective. Real joy is found in belonging to his family, depending on his providential care and trusting in his sovereign will. The hindrances that obstruct our path to joy may be removed one by one as we determine to move closer to our heavenly father.

People outside Christ may know ordinary joy, especially on occasions of celebration such as graduation, marriage, the birth of a baby, career advancement and success in some sporting achievement or the satisfaction that comes from a job well done. They may know ordinary joy in their relationships and experience that surprising joy that comes unexpectedly like a tax rebate, but this is not the same as the extraordinary joy that comes from belonging to Jesus. The pursuit of pleasure does not bring joy because pleasure and joy are very different things. As we witness people pursuing pleasure in profanity it is like watching children chasing fireflies in a minefield. This is something that should trouble us until we take the time to tell them about Jesus.

Those who believe in Christ should seize the day and not allow joy to evade them. The world says 'carpe diem' (seize the day) and means one thing but the Christian can say it and mean quite another thing altogether. The psalmist says, 'This is the day the LORD has made; let us rejoice and be glad in it' (Psalm 118:24). When we pick up this contemporary catch phrase we are acknowledging the truth conveyed by the psalmist and accepting his invitation to joyously enter into that truth.

John Piper supplies a comprehensive meditation on the theme of Christian joy:

But we also need tens of thousands of ordinary pastors, who are ravished with the extraordinary sovereignty of joy that belongs to and comes from God alone. And we need to rediscover Augustine's peculiar slant—a very biblical slant—on grace as the free gift of sovereign joy in God that frees us from the bondage of sin. We need to rethink our Reformed view of salvation so that every limb and every branch in the tree is coursing with the sap of Augustinian delight.

We need to make plain that *total depravity* is not just badness but blindness to beauty and deadness to joy; and *unconditional election* means that the completeness of our joy in Jesus was planned for us before we ever existed; and that *limited atonement* is the assurance that indestructible joy in God is infallibly secured for us by the blood of the covenant; and *irresistible grace* is the commitment and power of God's love to make sure we don't hold on to suicidal pleasures, and to set us free by the sovereign power of superior delights; and that the *perseverance of the saints* is the almighty work of God to keep us, through all affliction and suffering, for an inheritance of pleasures at God's right hand forever.

This note of sovereign, triumphant joy is a missing element in too much Reformed theology and Reformed worship. And it may be that the question we should pose

Chapter 2

ourselves is whether this is so because we have not experienced the triumph of sovereign joy in our lives.[3]

Notes on Chapter 2

1 The well known hymn by Philip Doddridge (1702–51)
2 'Je me presse de rire de tout, de peur d'être obligé d'en pleurer'. **Pierre-Augustin Caron De Beaumarchais** 1732–1799, *Le Barbier de Séville*, I.ii.
3 **John Piper,** *A Godward Life, Book Two* (Multnomah, 1999), pp. 81-82

Peace

'But the fruit of the Spirit is … peace …'

Peace is a universal and basic desire of all peoples whether they live in primitive or developed societies. In the history of Western civilisation we have records of many international peace treaties negotiated and ratified between independent sovereign states in the interests of their peoples. As a child at a matinee of a Western film I believe I shared in the young audience's sense of relief when the Sioux, Apache or some other tribe of 'Indians' smoked the peace pipe as a token that a peace deal was in the process of being clinched. Usually that sense of relief was soon displaced by a feeling of disappointment at the unfolding of a tragedy that served its own dramatic ends when that agreement was reneged and hostilities resumed with catastrophic consequences. Young, idealistic hearts yearn for peace and older, more cynical hearts have learned how elusive it can be.

A warring world

In the time of Christ too there were wars. The Roman armies were invading, conquering and subjugating other nations to their rule. Palestine at the time of Jesus was a place occupied by a foreign power. We still live in a world of wars. Palestine today is a place of conflict. Whether it is tribal gangs, military dictatorships, despotic rule, colonial rule, imperial authority, Marxism, Socialism, Fascism or democracy, no system of government is free from the threat of war. In every age and in every generation there have been wars motivated by religious, political, personal and economic reasons. We have seen the harrowing images of wars in the newspapers and on our television screens. We see how soldiers and civilians are slaughtered in some grand ideological cause. The images of conflict and strife are relayed into our living rooms and sadly we become all too accustomed to them. They no longer impact on us the way they should. Man's inhumanity to man is awful. Human rights are violated in many countries and atrocities such as genocide and holocausts are taking place as I write. It truly wrings the heart that men, women and children are subjected to wars and all the attendant evils of war such as famine, disease, torture and rape.

An elusive hope

If peace is such a desirable and precious thing why are human beings not capable of living in harmony in a peaceful world? Why do we have nuclear weapons of mass destruction? Why are there so many arms and munitions factories producing efficient killing machines? Why can disagreements between nations or within nations not be resolved peacefully? Why is there so much violence on our streets at night? Why is the world such an unsafe place? What is wrong with us? Surely it was not meant to be like this?

What is peace? Peace is more than the absence of war or freedom from civil disorder. Even in peacetime when a country is not at war many people are not at peace. Although highly desirable, peace seems to be virtually unobtainable for many people, as it is merely an elusive aspiration. Peace is not always related to external conditions and circumstances. A person might live in a peaceful environment and not be at peace within. Many people who have sought peace in quiet and tranquil environments have been disillusioned to learn that their new surroundings have not created the mental calm and serenity they longed for.

Some people think that humanity is evolving from a more primitive biological form of life and that as we develop we will learn to live in peace. But in many countries political structures and institutions are becoming increasingly corrupt. Corporate interests lead to the exploitation of the vulnerable. Violent crime and gangland murders are on the increase. Violence against children such as paedophilia is prevalent. Civil wars and international conflicts are raging in many countries. So that this utopian ideal that mankind is on an inexorable course to a developed world where social justice and civil order prevail is completely contradicted by the reality of the world in which we live. Our societies and the world, in general, are becoming increasingly dangerous. Man is not evolving, rather he is degenerating! Something has gone terribly wrong!

Freedom from spiritual disorder

Ultimately peace is rooted in freedom from spiritual disorder. Man was created to live in harmony with God and his fellow man. That was the act of *generation* that we call 'creation'. Then he rebelled against God and that was the act of *degeneration* that we call 'The Fall'. Man's greatest need now is for that act of *regeneration* that we call 'redemption', 'new birth' or 'reconciliation'. Man was designed to live at peace with God. But humanity has become estranged from God. People in their degenerate state are no longer at peace with God. People are at war with God. That is the teaching of the Bible. People are not in need of spiritual renewal; rather they are in need of spiritual rebirth. God desires sinners to receive salvation, safety and security.

The cause of conflict

Sin prevents us from living in harmony with God and each other. Our natural instinct is to repay evil with evil but Peter tells us that this is not the way Christians ought to behave, 'Do not repay evil with evil or insult with insult, but with blessing' (1 Peter 3:9). Jesus said, 'If someone strikes you on one cheek, turn to him the other also' (Luke 6:29). Yet we think this is naive and unworkable. We say it is not realistic; we find it difficult to imagine a positive outcome if that principle was applied, for example, in the Middle-East or Northern Ireland! Perhaps I am a hopeless idealist but I believe in taking God at his Word, irrespective of the outcome. But I also believe that the outcome will be good when we obey God. The vicious cycle of retaliation, reprisal and the lust for revenge have never achieved peace! The path to peace is found in following biblical principles. But it is not possible for those estranged from God to endorse and enact those principles unless they first undergo a radical transformation of heart.

If we are to be at peace with God and live in a state of friendliness with our Creator he must first become our Saviour. That is how we are reconciled to God, through Christ. We must acknowledge this estrangement and enmity, and realise our sinful condition before a holy and just God. It is in confessing that sinfulness to him and accepting his death as a substitution for the death we deserve for our sins that we are born again of the Spirit of God. In this sense we are, by the Holy Spirit's prompting and

Christ's provision, making our peace with God and thereby re-establishing friendly relations with him. This is how we come to make peace with God - by agreeing to end the war or quarrel that commenced with Adam but continued in our hearts through our attitudes and actions. It is God who makes provision for us in this way so that we might avail of the work of Christ in seeing it appropriated in our lives. Jesus is our peace offering in that he is God the Father's propitiatory or conciliatory gift to those who come to him in faith and repentance believing in his finished work at Calvary. It is by grace alone, through faith alone, in Christ alone that we have redemption by his blood. Grace is God's unmerited favour to us as hell-deserving sinners. There is no residual virtue or moral excellence in any individual that causes God to redeem such a person by virtue of their goodness. It is only those who trust in Christ's goodness that are saved and at peace with God. This is the great physician's prescription for having peace with God, which in turn enables us to live peacefully with others.

It may be impossible to live peacefully with everyone in a hostile world but that is not a loophole to be used to justify not trying to do so! We are to do all that we can to live in harmony with others. Paul instructs, 'If it is possible, as far as it depends on you, live at peace with everyone. Do not take revenge' (Romans 12:18–19). As we obey God's commands he will enable us by supplying the supernatural grace needed to bear the fruit of peace.

In the world of economics there is a concept known as a 'peace dividend' whereby public money becomes available when defence spending is reduced. In a sense this happens too in the spiritual realm, when enmity with God ends there is a sense of relief and a release of blessing that was otherwise withheld. God can now invest in the one who turns to him in humility.

A modern illustration

I recently saw a television documentary about changes in sexual attitudes since the Second World War. In the course of the programme a true story was told about a newly married couple who became separated because of the war, as many couples did. The husband went to fight on the European Continent and the wife stayed at home. They did not have any children.

Some time after they said farewell and parted (say about two years) the young lady had sex with another man and she became pregnant. It was obvious to all that the father of her child was not her husband. His sister informed the young soldier of his wife's adultery. The husband was broken-hearted and sued for divorce and the wife was devastated that her one indiscretion (for that is what it was) had such a tragic outcome. She had deceived her husband and broken a sacred trust in that dangerous and foolish liaison. She loved him and he loved her but now all the promise of a happy future together was thrown away. Neither of them married again. She lived a life of regret for what might have been, and he secretly cherished a love for her in his heart. Time elapsed until fifty years had passed and the couple had no contact with each other during that time. She had hoped he would forgive her and he had hoped she would say she was sorry.

Then one day out of the blue the man made contact with the woman by letter and she replied to him. They confessed their love for each other. After all those years they were still in love. They arranged to meet and decided to remarry. They were at last united in love. It is a wonderful but very sad story. They had wasted their lives only to find in the end what they had in the beginning! They were at peace with each other.

An olive branch

In this case the woman had done something very wrong and the man did not, I think, give her opportunity to repent. With God, however, we are given an opportunity to repent even though we have offended him greatly in our wrongdoing. Will we not respond to his overtures of true love, when he desires to be gracious to us? Will we not repent and be at peace with the lover of our souls? It is only when we are at peace *with* God that we come to know the peace *of* God. Paul puts it to us this way: 'Therefore, since we have been justified through faith, we have peace with God through our Lord Jesus Christ' (Romans 5:1). We are not naturally at peace with God because sin broke the peaceful relationship of Eden. This is why the world is in trouble. Many people are desperately searching for peace. They try to find it in the pursuit of pleasure, serial sexual relationships and entertainment. Many find their quest for this elusive quality of life leads them to use substances such as alcohol and other drugs. Others chase after financial security in the vain hope that it can fill the aching void in their souls that longs for peace with thrills and things that are for sale.

A restless quest

Millions have sought (and are still seeking today) peace with God in the wrong place and in the wrong way. Peace with God is not found in religious ritual. Peace with God is not found through good works. Peace with God is not found through the giving of one's possessions. Peace with God is not obtained through a monastic or cloistered life of asceticism.

However, there is no peace apart from God. The prophet Isaiah talks of this restlessness among the 'wicked'. '"Peace, peace, to those far and near," says the LORD. "And I will heal them." But the wicked are like the tossing sea, which cannot rest, whose waves cast up mire and mud. "There is no peace," says my God, "for the wicked"' (Isaiah 57:19–21). There is restlessness in the human soul that can only be stilled by God. Augustine said: 'Thou hast made us for Thyself and our hearts are restless, until they find their rest in Thee.' Man out of relationship with God, man in sin, is restless, wretched and unhappy. Here in Isaiah 57, as elsewhere in Scripture, the term 'wicked' does not necessarily refer specifically to those who commit appalling acts of evil but rather to the godless in general. In contemporary parlance we are talking about the secularist, the atheist and the agnostic, the one who is indifferent about religion as well as those hostile to the Christian faith. In biblical terms the petty pilferer of paper clips and the paedophile are alike 'wicked'. Stated in these stark terms the depravity of sin is quite shocking. Pilfering is really a symptom of sinfulness in the same way as paedophilia is also a symptom of the same condition. Whereas the former is a slight presentation of that inner malady the latter is a blatant manifestation of the extent of the disease when it takes hold. Some have fallen much further than others but we have all fallen. Certainly there are degrees of wickedness but these are degrees of quality rather than differences in kind. A sinner is a sinner. If we never come to realise that, we never come to fully appreciate God's grace. So the godless are lost and wandering aimlessly or pursuing wrong goals that they think will ultimately lead to peace. But there is good news; Christ came to bring us peace. He died for sinners.

You see, at just the right time, when we were still powerless, Christ died for the ungodly. Very rarely will anyone die for a righteous man, though for a good man someone might possibly dare to die. But God demonstrates his own love for us in this: While we were still sinners, Christ died for us. Since we have now been justified by his blood, how much more shall we be saved from God's wrath through him! (Romans 5:6–9).

The cross of Christ has spanned that great chasm between a sinful people and a holy God. The great divide has been bridged and for those who wish to cross to the other side there is only one way. There is no other route to heaven. Jesus said: 'I am the way and the truth and the life. No-one comes to the Father except through me' (John 14:6). He is the path to peace.

He is the source of peace

The work of Christ, when it has been appropriated in the life of the person who yields to him in faith and repentance, is the way to peace. Paul expressed this emphatically and eloquently to the Ephesian believers:

But now in Christ Jesus you who once were far away have been brought near through the blood of Christ. For he himself is our peace, who has made the two one and has destroyed the barrier, the dividing wall of hostility, by abolishing in his flesh the law with its commandments and regulations. His purpose was to create in himself one new man out of the two, thus making peace, and in this one body to reconcile both of them to God through the cross, by which he put to death their hostility. He came and preached peace to you who were far away and peace to those who were near (Ephesians 2:13–17).

Estrangement is replaced with intimacy, distance with closeness, barriers with blessing, hostility with hope, wrath with reconciliation and perplexity with peace. As H. L. Goudge said, 'Grace is the free favour of God; peace is the condition which results from its reception.' We must not think of grace only as the once off transaction of salvation. Sustaining grace is needed hour by hour. That daily peace is possessed through daily prayer. When we have peace *with* God obstructions to the peace *of* God are removed and that channel of communication is open for the blessing of peace. Anxieties prevent us from experiencing peace. As Christians we need that awareness of God's sovereignty to dispel fear. Peace prospers in hearts that prove the providential care of God and thereby learn to trust. Our God is the supreme sovereign. He is a powerful yet personal God. Consider his omnipotence and omniscience and let the peace of God that passes all understanding reign in your hearts.

Christ is himself the fruit of God's prophetic promise given in Isaiah, '... he will be called Wonderful Counsellor, Mighty God, Everlasting Father, Prince of Peace' (9:6). He is 'Peace' in name and nature! This great title speaks of the greatest need of the human heart, the need for peace with God. The birth of Jesus was announced as the fulfilment of that promise of peace: 'Glory to God in the highest, and on earth peace to men on whom his favour rests' (Luke 2:14). Could anything be more welcome news in an age of unrest? J.C. Ryle said, 'there will be no universal peace until the prince of peace rules'. To this I would like to add that we can never know personal peace until the prince of peace rules in our hearts. Jesus taught peace and ministered peace to others through his gracious actions. When a sick woman touched the hem of his garment with that finger of faith he said, 'Go in peace and be freed from your suffering' (Mark 5:34). When Christ spoke of the Holy Spirit who would come to comfort the believer after his departure he put it like this, 'Peace I leave with you; my peace I give you' (John 14:27).

A reigning resident

God bought that peace through Christ's blood (Colossians 1:19–20) and he will produce it as fruit in the life of the Christian where the Holy Spirit resides and reigns. He is in a sense not only the author of peace but also the arbitrator of that peace. If we think of an arbitrator, not so much as an independent third party (as that would not be true of Christ), but rather as one who works toward the settlement of a dispute, then we have a picture of Christ. There are two parties in dispute, God and us, and the work of Jesus brought about the resolution to that dispute, not through an agreed compromise that was negotiated but by the sacrifice of atonement offered. We must allow this peace of Christ to rule in our hearts (Colossians 3:15). He takes away our anxieties and replaces them with the assurance of his presence, provision and power. In a world of many pressures he has provided peace to those who will follow him. God takes away our spiritual confusion and gives us comfort in Christ. This is peace and there is no other peace besides. The world may offer counterfeit attractions but those who try to possess peace outside of Christ will eventually and ultimately find that they are actually impoverished. As John Owen said, 'Nothing can give perfect peace of conscience with God but what can make atonement for sin. And whoever attempts it in any other way but by virtue of that atonement will never attain it, in this world or hereafter.'

When I was a teenager I remember making a poster for the local Christian bookshop with the words 'No God, No Peace; Know God, Know Peace.' I do not remember where I had picked up this slogan but I had it written in large bold letters on the inside cover of my first Bible. I come back to it now after thirty years as a succinct statement that sums up what we are dealing with here.

The Peace of God

Spurgeon said: 'It is in the way of truth that real peace is found' and this too is the message of the Master. Jesus said: 'I have told you these things, so that in me you may have peace. In this world you will have trouble. But take heart! I have overcome the world' (John 16:33). Peace *with* God, based as it is on our trust in his finished work of salvation at Calvary, is positional and unchanging. It is a peace that comes from being in Christ. Peace *with* God should not, however, be limited to our position in Christ. In other words, when we have peace *with* God we should feel peaceful! The peace *of* God should be our daily experience. This is what Paul advised: 'Do not be anxious about anything, but in everything, by prayer and petition, with thanksgiving, present your requests to God. And the peace of God, which transcends all understanding, will guard your hearts and your minds in Christ Jesus' (Philippians 4:6–7). Peace is not some kind of holy feeling that we experience exclusively in church; rather it is a lifestyle based on the repose of a soul rooted in God and resting in his grace. Thus the Christian may have this peace in all circumstances, even when things appear to be not going well. We must not allow anxiety to rob us of that precious peace. We can know peace in financial struggles. We can know peace when we have health issues and concerns. We can know that transcendent and triumphant peace when storms are raging all about.

Peace with Others

God wants to instil peace in our hearts and he also desires to see that peace promoted and perpetuated. So what is God's formula for this kind of peace? How are we to preserve it and promote it? The Holy Spirit prompts prayer, produces thanksgiving and gives faith as a means of securing and sustaining peace in our hearts and in our relationships and it is by these means that peace prospers. The recipe for peace is not some kind of mysterious or secret formula. Paul told the Ephesians what ingredients were required for peace, 'As a prisoner for the Lord, then, I urge you to live a life worthy of the calling you have received. Be completely humble and gentle; be patient, bearing with one another in love. Make every effort to keep the unity of the Spirit through the bond of peace' (Ephesians 4:1–3). So we are to be humble because arrogance and pride spoil peace. We are to be gentle because aggression and hostility ruin peace. We are to be patient because impatience and restlessness stir up problems and peace will not thrive in that environment. We are to bear with one another not just in some kind of detached philosophical way, but 'in love'. Love is the perfect environment in which humility, gentleness and patience flourish and produce the fruit of peace.

Breaking down barriers

If we allow the Holy Spirit's peace to rule in our hearts, then barriers between believers will be broken down. Our obligations to promote peace extend beyond the confines of our Christian communities. The writer to the Hebrews instructs us to 'Make every effort to live in peace with all men' (Hebrews 12:14). We should jealously guard and covet such harmonious relationships and do everything possible to nurture peace with those who belong to Christ and those who do not. This is not only right but it is also wise, in fact what is right is always wise. As James says, 'But the wisdom that comes from heaven is first of all pure; then peace-loving, considerate, submissive, full of mercy and good fruit, impartial and sincere. Peacemakers who sow in peace raise a harvest of righteousness' (James

3:17–18). So we ought, for our own sakes and for God's glory, endeavour to live in peaceful coexistence with our fellow human beings in our personal relationships, in our inter-community relationships and in our international relationships. We should never do anything that would infringe peace for that is contrary to what God wants from us. It may take considerable effort to keep the peace, refrain from conflict and prevent strife but we cannot shirk our responsibility in this regard merely because it is difficult. It is not so much, after all, about what we are *able* to do; rather it is about what we are *enabled* to do in the power of the Holy Spirit. Peaceable people are a joy to God because he wants us to be disposed to peace. The 'might is right' philosophy, which is seen in many personal, national and international scenarios is deeply offensive to God who said: 'Blessed are the peacemakers, for they will be called sons of God' (Matthew 5:9). Remember that Jesus spoke these words in his own country when it was occupied by a foreign military power. Many of his hearers (even perhaps the closest of his disciples) hoped that he would be their emancipator or at least the catalyst that would spearhead the desired liberation and change in the political landscape. He disabused any potential conspirators of the notion that his mission was anything other than one of mercy, love and peace. The message of peace needs to be preached and practised in this world today, especially by those who profess to be disciples of Jesus.

Riding the crest of the waves

It is by living as God intends for us to live that we find real, meaningful peace, purpose and contentment. Recently as I walked along the beach I watched the huge Atlantic waves pounding the shore and thought that waves are only a surface thing. I watched several surfers riding the crests of those waves and I thought, beneath the surface the sea is undisturbed. This is how it ought to be in the life of the Christian. Circumstances may create waves but deep down we remain undisturbed because our hearts are at peace with God. If only we could see those circumstances as surfers see waves; as great opportunities to practice and hone our skills and master the conditions. What a difference it would make!

Referring to Jesus Paul tells the Ephesians, 'For he himself is our peace'

(2:14). Those who know Christ as their Saviour have a claim on that peace. The psalmist tells us that peace is the outcome of loving the Scriptures: 'Great peace have they who love your law' (119:165). We need to continue to cultivate a sincere appreciation of God's Word in a cynical generation. It is in loving and living that Word that we inherit and inhabit peace. Often we discover ourselves in the narratives of Scripture and learn the lessons of the patriarchs and prophets. We come to understand ourselves as part of God's plan and live in peace with those purposes. Peace is *obtained* when relationship commences with God and it is *retained* as relationship continues with God. Thus the peace of God resides and reigns in our hearts as the Spirit of God dwells within us and produces fruit for our good and his glory. We must permit this peace to be present and pre-eminent in our lives. In doing this we are taking Paul's counsel to the Colossians, 'Let the peace of Christ rule in your hearts' (3:15). What good fruit the Holy Spirit longs to produce in us to enrich our lives, fruit such as love, joy and peace.

We have already alluded to the fact that many people seem to think that peace may be obtained by changing their circumstances (relationship, relocation, change of career, etc.), but biblical peace is a supernatural power at work in the life of the believer to produce contentment in all circumstances. How often we allow anxieties and fears to deprive us of the peace that God desires for us. As Christians we ought not to expect immunity from problems but we can expect the comfort that comes from knowing Christ at such times. The believer has the constant companionship of Christ. As Jesus promised, 'I am with you always, to the very end of the age' (Matthew 28:20). It is interesting to note that Paul begins all his correspondence to the churches and to individuals with the words 'Grace and peace to you'. We may tend to overlook this as merely a customary form of salutation in correspondence. But I think it would be quite wrong to think of these greetings as no more than a conventional introduction to the ensuing correspondence. On the contrary, these words are weighty and have great significance. I do not think it would be exegetically fallacious to emphasise the order of those words as they appear in the texts of Scripture. In other words the fact that 'grace' precedes 'peace' in the greetings is significant because real peace results only from God's grace in our lives!

The essential meaning of the Hebrew word for peace, *sálom*, used in the Old Testament is 'completeness', 'soundness' or 'well-being'. It is used in a variety of contexts, including physical security, such as when David says, 'I will lie down and sleep in peace, for you alone, O LORD, make me dwell in safety' (Psalm 4:8). However, it is also used to mean spiritual security and is closely associated with righteousness and truth. We see this in Psalm 85:10, 'Love and faithfulness meet together; righteousness and peace kiss each other.' Or Isaiah 48:18, 'If only you had paid attention to my commands, your peace would have been like a river, your righteousness like the waves of the sea.' In this latter verse we see that peace is the outcome of adhering to the truth of God's Word. The Messianic hope of the Old Testament rested in the advent of the Prince of Peace, which comes to fruition in the New Testament in the person of Christ. Christ is peace and he confers peace on those who trust in him. His disciples are harbingers of peace (see Luke 10:5ff).

In the New Testament the Greek word *eiréné* carries with it all the significance of the Old Testament word *sálom*, but almost always has a spiritual nuance and is closely connected with other significant words such as 'grace' (Romans 1:7), 'life' (Romans 8:6) and 'righteousness' (Romans 14:17). It is a benediction blessing bestowed on the believer (see 1 Thessalonians 5:23 and Hebrews 10:20ff).

The result of reconciliation

Biblical peace is about harmonious relationships between God and humans as well as within humanity itself. It is the outcome of the gospel, which brings about that reconciliation. Peace is the result of that new sense of belonging to God. The inward feeling of peace (Philippians 4:7) desired by so many is the result of being at peace with God (Romans 5:1; Colossians 1:20). It is a transcendent peace that is qualitatively different to the kind of peace that is obtainable outside Christ (John 14:27). Peace in human relationships is the new kingdom order, ideally exemplified in the church, for which Christ died (Ephesians 2). It is the work of the Holy Spirit (Galatians 5:22) who has entrusted those who belong to him with the great responsibility of fostering and developing peace wherever possible (Ephesians 4:3; Hebrews 12:14). We must work to eradicate strife and dissension and promote the harmony that God desires (Romans 14: 19) because it reflects something of who he is (1 Corinthians 14: 33). He is the Prince of Peace (Isaiah 9:6).

Worry deprives us of the peace we desire. It is rooted in a feeling of powerlessness to alter circumstances, but peace is found in resting under the control of Christ and the power of the Holy Spirit. Jesus taught his disciples that they should not worry about the things of tomorrow because they deprive us of the blessings of today (Matthew 6:25–34). We can all say this is easier said than done, but in doing so are we saying that the teaching of Christ is impractical? We need to be emotionally, intellectually and spiritually transformed (Romans 12:2) so that we can actualise our inheritance in Christ.

A song for our times

Psalm 46 is a refreshing wellspring of peace to our souls. It is a song of holy confidence, a song of faith in troubled times. It is a precious psalm and a perfect meditation on peace. It speaks to us in a way that is meaningful because as Christians we do not live in ivory towers that protect us from trouble. However, in such times we must not lose our spiritual bearings. We have been called to live to glorify him through peaceful confidence in Christ. As we face present difficulties and future uncertainty, this is a song we must learn to sing if we are to come through such times, triumphant in our God.

The psalms were not written in a vacuum; rather they were conceived in the crucible of the real life experiences of the people of God. They are not the detached, theoretical reflections of religious philosophers upon life. They are the groaning of real believers in the midst of real problems, in the real world in which they were called upon to glorify God. They are the praises wrung out of real situations in which the true God manifested his power and ministered his perfect peace.

Troubled times

This psalm came out of a situation in which the people of God found themselves in troubled times and the very first verse lays that fact before us, 'God is our refuge and strength, an ever present help in trouble'. It is a psalm in which the contemplation focuses upon God's relationship to his people in troubled times. Not only so, but there is, perhaps, a sense of anticipation of greater troubles to come, 'Therefore we will not fear, though the earth give way, and the mountains fall into the heart of the sea.' Whatever may happen, God is still our refuge and strength!

Whatever precise historical setting gave birth to this psalm, it is a song of peace in the midst of perplexing times. As such it is very relevant today. In times of upheaval and opposition to the people of God we need to reflect on the theme of peace presented to us in this psalm. However calamitous the situation may appear God provided the believer with security and peace.

Here we have not only a great theological truth but also a personal statement. The psalmist does not say that 'God is *a* refuge and strength' even though that is true. He goes further and says, 'God is *our* refuge and strength'. More than that, it is not only a *personal* statement; it is also a *plural* statement. In other words he is not merely saying that this is his unique and exceptional experience, but that it is the common experience of covenant relationship with God. This is crucial to understanding the message of the psalm. In verse 7 we have the same emphasis, 'The Lord of hosts is with *us*; the God of Jacob is *our* refuge' (NKJV). The psalmist is speaking on behalf of those who have entered into covenant relationship with God, those who may be rightly called his people. The covenant promise given to Abraham was renewed through Jacob. So this psalm is speaking *of* God's people and *to* God's people about the marvellous effect that relationship with him has upon the human heart. So the basic assumption of the psalmist is that this is a hymn of those who are in covenant relationship with God. This is seen in the next stanza, which speaks of 'the city of God, the holy place where the Most High dwells' (v. 4). Only those who have come to Jesus, the mediator of the new covenant, are citizens of that city (Hebrews 12:22–24). The Old Testament passport was gained through messianic anticipation, whereas our hope rests in the historical reality of the cross. Thus the believer can say 'God … OUR refuge … OUR strength' because believers are citizens of Zion, the city of the living God! It is a profound and personal statement that indicates a dynamic and living union with God.

Chapter 3

Seek the Saviour

Strangers to the blood of the new covenant are strangers to the regenerating power of the Holy Spirit who produces the fruit of transcendent peace, which is presented in this psalm. Such strangers need to seek the Saviour by whose merit alone they can become citizens of heaven. Then and only then can they join with their fellow citizens in saying 'God is *our* refuge and strength'!

Changeless certainty

This psalm, like the Bible generally, assumes that God exists. It does not seek to prove the reality of God's existence through argument. It simply declares the reality of the being of God. This is a significant element of the meditation of the psalm. We ought to consider the possible distresses that might come to pass in the lives of the people of God as human beings in this world, and the peculiar afflictions that may befall the believer in the context of that changeless certainty. If we are to know real peace we need to allow our minds and hearts to be gripped and moved with the soundness of that kind of spiritual perspective!

Although the mountains may pass away the God who made the mountains and the sea is not affected by the changes in his creation. He is changeless! This is the language faith will speak wherever faith is present. The writer to the Hebrews says, 'And without faith it is impossible to please God, because anyone who comes to him must believe that he exists and that he rewards those who earnestly seek him' (11:6). It is in believing *that* he is, knowing *who* he is and belonging to him that we come to know peace as fruit of the Holy Spirit. He is the eternal God, creator of heaven and earth; the one who sustains the universe. He is the absolute sovereign who does according to his good and perfect will. He is self-sufficient, not dependent on his creatures, not frustrated by their whims, and it is in him that we place our confidence.

In another psalm God invites us to call on him in times of trouble: 'Call upon me in the day of trouble; I will deliver you, and you shall glorify me' (Psalm 50:15). Clearly the Bible acknowledges that the people of God are not exempt from trouble. Yet our peace comes from knowing Christ as Lord and Saviour. Thus we can say with Paul, 'Who shall separate us from the love of Christ? Shall tribulation, or distress, or persecution ... in all these things we are more than conquerors through him who loved us' (Romans 8:35–37, NKJV). In chapter twelve Paul speaks of being 'patient in affliction' (Romans 12:12, NKJV). John, in writing the book of Revelation, understood tribulation to be so much part and parcel of the Christian experience that he describes himself as 'your brother, and companion in tribulation'(1:9). Yet peace is possible in any situation because God is our refuge and strength. He is our retreat in troubled times. We can flee to him when we are under pressure!

God is never an indifferent spectator to the trials of his people. In Isaiah we read, 'In all their distress he too was distressed, and the angel of his presence saved them. In his love and mercy he redeemed them; he lifted them up and carried them all the days of old' (Isaiah 63:9). This is the character of God's relationship with his people, in all times and in all situations. Surely this thought produces inner peace.

A compelling conclusion

When we in faith can say that God exists and when we can describe our relationship to God in these personal terms, we too can say that he is a strong and safe retreat and a very present help in trouble. The inexorable logic inherent in Psalm 46 compels us to conclude, 'Therefore we will not fear' (v. 2). We resolve, in the light of our understanding of his power and care that we will not be consumed by emotions that make us fearful and deprive us of peace. Our fears and anxieties not only deprive us of peace but they discredit God. Fear may fill the hearts of those who are ignorant of God or indifferent to him but peace should be the possession of Christ's disciples.

The earth, the sea and the mountains symbolise all that appears permanent and stable. Dynasties, nations and empires have risen and fallen into the earth only to have their ruins excavated by archaeologists! What is more stable than the mountains? Great cities have been destroyed by war but the mountains survive. They existed before civilisations, political systems and institutions. Poets have written of their beauty and scientists have studied their geological grandeur. What is a greater symbol of permanence, order, continuity and regularity than the ebb and flow of the sea? The psalmist is saying that the relationship God has with his people is the most permanent thing of all. Though all that appears permanent in this world is shaken, I will not be deprived of peace because my God is seated above the circle of the earth and is in control and he cares for me! Astonishing! Even when his creation is altered his relationship to his people does not change irrespective of what may change in the physical realm.

The tremendous message of this mighty psalm is that if the greatest calamities do not fill me with fear neither will anything lesser disturb my peace! My God is bigger than the problem and he does not change!

There is a time coming when the things spoken of in these verses will happen and those who do not know Jesus Christ as Lord and Saviour will call for the rocks of the mountains to fall on them and bury them! We do not fear that impending judgement because we have found our refuge in him! O the bliss of eternal security in Christ! Almighty God in mercy has sent forth his gospel in his Son and we must call on people to repent and seek the Lord while he may be found. The Christian hope is not merely human optimism; rather it is based on a sure foundation. We can depend on him because he is dependable. God is our refuge and strength and we have inner peace through implicit trust in his power and love. The fruit of peace is evidence of Christian maturity.

It is well with my soul

The author of the hymn, *When Peace like a River*, Horatio G. Spafford (1828–1888) experienced great personal tragedy. But it was out of the crucible of very painful experience that one of the greatest Christian hymns ever written was penned. He was a successful member of the legal profession in Chicago. He was married with four daughters and an active member of the Presbyterian Church. He was a friend and supporter of D. L. Moody and other evangelical leaders of that time.

His substantial property investments were destroyed in the great Chicago fire of 1871. In these depressing circumstances he decided to take his wife and children on a holiday to England in order to refresh their spirits. He planned to be involved in the Moody and Sankey meeting there. However, he was detained on urgent business and his wife and daughters (Tanetta, Maggie, Annie and Bessie) went ahead as planned. Horatio planned to follow them as soon as possible. In the middle of the Atlantic Ocean in November 1873 the ship on which his wife and four daughters were travelling, the *S.S. Ville du Harve*, collided with another ship and sank in twelve minutes. Amazingly his wife and a few others survived but all four of his beloved daughters were drowned along with 222 other people. He travelled by ship to meet his wife in Cardiff and was standing on deck when the ship passed the place where the tragedy had occurred. He was inspired to write the words of that now famous hymn 'It Is Well With My Soul'. Considering the context in which it was conceived let us recall those wonderful words.

When peace, like a river, attendeth my way,
When sorrows, like sea billows, roll,
Whatever my lot, thou hast taught me to say,
It is well, it is well with my soul.

Though Satan should buffet, though trials should come,
Let this blest assurance control,
That Christ has regarded my helpless estate,
And has shed his own blood for my soul.

My sin—O the bliss of this glorious thought!—
My sin, not in part, but the whole,
Is nailed to his cross, and I bear it no more:
Praise the Lord, praise the Lord, O my soul!

For me be it Christ, be it Christ hence to live!
If Jordan above me shall roll,
No pang shall be mine, for in death as in life
Thou wilt whisper thy peace to my soul.

But, Lord, 'tis for thee, for thy coming we wait;
The sky, not the grave, is our goal;
O trump of the Angel! O voice of the Lord!
Blessèd hope! blessèd rest of my soul.[1]

Chapter 3

Notes on Chapter 3

1 **Paul E.G. Cook and Graham Harrison** (eds), *Christian Hymns* (Bridgend, Evangelical Movement of Wales, 1977).

Patience

'But the fruit of the Spirit is ... patience ...'

God intended that mankind should live in harmonious relationship with his fellow human beings. We do not live in isolation, and it is inevitable that in our relationships (filial, occupational, recreational, societal, etc.) there will be times when we irritate one another. How we handle these times of annoyance and frustration is an important matter that challenges all believers. Some people are easily irritated whereas others appear to be quite placid by nature. Whether we are inherently irritable or paragons of patience, we need to understand that patience as fruit of the Spirit is supernaturally endowed rather than a matter of temperament. Are we easily angered? Even if our anger is justifiable, our responses must be righteous, not just reactionary.

We have already seen that God is the example par excellence of love, joy and peace; so too he is the supreme model of patience in his relationship with humanity in general and with his people in particular. God has restrained his righteous anger against a rebellious race. One day he will judge the living and the dead but that will not be an act of impatience by a frustrated God. It is the inexorable destiny of humanity. Those whose sins are judged in Christ will inherit the eternal reward reserved for them in heaven and those who still bear their own sin will be cast into hell, a place of conscious and eternal torment. We must never avoid this biblical truth.

For now, God is longsuffering and desires that we too should be longsuffering with each other. The word longsuffering is derived from the Greek, *makrothumia*, a compound word, which joins the word for 'anger' or 'temper' (*thumos*) and the word for 'slow' or 'long' (*makro*). In other words it speaks of handling anger slowly! This same notion of God is represented in the Old Testament by the Hebrew word *árék* (long or slow). This in effect means that patience puts the brakes on anger. Anger may, however, be expressed in a controlled manner. Patience, therefore, is listed as spiritual fruit in marked contrast to acts of the sinful nature which includes 'fits of rage' (Galatians 5:20). This insight may help us to apply patience in our daily experience. Rather than feeling that we live in a world where it is impossible to be patient with particular circumstances and people, we should begin to think of the opportunities this presents for us to manifest the fruit of patience. In doing this we glorify God, and the converse is equally true that in being impatient we discredit our faith, hinder harmony in the church and put an obstacle in the path of effective evangelism.

Repentance and restoration

God's patience is an expression of his love because it permits opportunity for repentance, restitution and restoration. A real understanding and appreciation of God's patience can help us to be patient with others. Patience involves a willingness to forgive. Even when people repeatedly hurt us we are called to habitually forgive. In the parable of the unmerciful servant (Matthew 18:21–35) there is a marked contrast in the way the first servant was treated and the way in which he in turn treated his fellow servant. When the king desired to settle outstanding accounts, he summoned a debtor who owed ten thousand talents, a vast sum that a servant could not possibly repay. As he was unable to pay, the intention of his master to sell him, his wife, and all his goods to offset the debt was a terrible prospect. He begged for patience and promised to repay the debt, but the master took pity on him and cancelled the money owed. In this his difficulties were resolved in an act of great magnanimity. Yet when this man dealt with a fellow servant who owed him one hundred denarii he grabbed him and choked him and demanded full repayment of the debt. This was the equivalent of one hundred days wages and as such was trivial in comparison to his debt that had been cancelled. This fellow servant also begged for patience, but alas, his pleas did not penetrate the hard heart of one that had benefited from the patience of his master, and the unfortunate man was thrown into prison. This act distressed the other servants who reported the matter to their master. The master again summoned the servant whose great debt had been cancelled and chastised him for his failure to emulate the patience and mercy of his master. We must have hearts like our heavenly master's and from those hearts should issue patience as an act of appreciation for his great patience to us whose debt of sin he has cancelled.

Patience in perspective

The cross puts everything else into proper perspective. There we see the majestic portrayal of God's perfect patience. There is no better example of the prolonged restraint of anger. Christ was falsely accused, betrayed, deserted, beaten, mocked, taunted, humiliated, spat on and nailed to a cross. In the light of such provocation he displayed divine patience and in doing this he set the standard that defines and describes true, perfect patience. From this we learn that we need supernatural strength to portray patience as fruit of the Spirit. His treatment of us is the model of how we ought to treat others.

Impatience hinders fellowship with God. Believers need to express their gratitude for Christ's patience by being patient with others. This parable was prompted by Peter's question to Christ 'Lord, how many times shall I forgive my brother when he sins against me? Up to seven times?' (Matthew 18:21). Rabbinical teaching of the time would have taught to forgive three times so Peter's suggestion of seven times must have seemed to him to be quite magnanimous. But Christ's answer multiplies Peter's notion of forgiveness by a numeral that is itself a multiple of Peter's suggestion. Clearly Christ was telling Peter that his understanding of forgiveness was ridiculously inadequate in true spiritual terms. The point is not that forgiveness should expire when it has reached a certain quota but that the principle of forgiveness ought to be a matter of lifestyle, a habitual and sincere expression of patience. As such this parable was a corrective to the prevailing religious view of the day and I believe that in this, Christ is calling on true Christians today to exercise patient forgiveness far in excess of the standards and expectations of religious duty. Even legalism requires patience and forgiveness, but love demands more. This is the fruit of the Spirit that we call patience.

It may be helpful for us to have some degree of self-awareness that enables us to avoid those situations that cause us to lose our patience. Ultimately, however, we need to be able to manage our emotions effectively rather than trying to create an 'ideal' environment that excludes people and situations that are potentially threatening to our patience. Besides, such a private little world would be very thinly populated. Even if we inhabited such a world on our own we might still have to face our impatience with climate and other conditions and even impatience with ourselves!

A precious quality

In spite of the fact that we live in a world where we have instant access to much that we desire, there may be times in a person's life when aspirations and ambitions are frustrated. There are many times in people's lives when there are unexpected delays. Events are postponed much to our annoyance and frustration. In business, personnel and products can be delayed or late with the result that time is lost and the achievement of certain goals are hindered and targets have to be deferred. It is obvious that patience is a virtue that is often needed. Yet in today's world it is a quality that is becoming increasingly scarce. Many people seem to be fixated with fulfilling the ambitions of their personal agendas. There seems to be a ruthless impatience in so many areas of life. There is impatience in marriage and family relationships. There is increasing impatience in the service sector amongst consumers and providers alike. Motorists are impatient. Television interviewers are frequently so impatient that they often do not allow their interviewees to answer the questions they have put. This reflects a more general attitude in society. It has been anonymously said: 'Patience is a quality that is most needed when it is exhausted.' It is certainly something that is very precious and much needed in our human relationships.

Peddlers of patience

The world appreciates patience and sees it as a desirable virtue. It is generally understood to be something noble. Some people are willing to pay for it and there are plenty of charlatans and gurus involved in the business of selling it. If you were to enter the word 'patience' to any of the Internet search-engines you would come up with some extraordinary hits including sites that offer to sell patience! One site that I visited had a long list of sought-after virtues including patience. Some of these sites offer 'Embodying Divinity Sessions' whatever that might be! These impostors claim to work with the soul and spirit to help people to remove obstacles that prevent them from experiencing the divine attribute they wish to develop. Whatever their motives may be; and I suspect that they are merely exploiting people for financial gain; they are offering false hope to needy people. Those who trade in this way are profiting from people who are crying out for graces that can only be supplied by the Holy Spirit. This seriously grieves the Holy Spirit and those who trade in spiritual things will find their very souls in jeopardy. The faceless people behind one such site said that they 'work to recalibrate and realign all of your energy bodies and fields so that you may embody the trait that you wish to express.' As the saying goes, 'a fool and his money are easily parted.' The astonishing thing about this kind of operation is that people actually buy into it. The challenge for the Christian is to wake up to the reality of this and to stop being ashamed of the gospel.

Dicing with the devil

Some of these frauds claim that they are merely offering to facilitate a self-healing process. They suggest that one's own soul and spirit do the healing and energy work. Some of these websites list the most popular attributes requested by 'clients'. The word 'clients' gives the nefarious swindle a professional veneer. These conniving scoundrels cheat people out of their money. One site that I consulted charges $50 per attribute. In other words the fruit of the Spirit can be purchased for $450. The tricksters involved in this racket claim to transmit the energy requested within four days after they receive your order. Sufficient time for the money of the gullible to be safely pocketed by the con men, I suggest! Such people are dicing with the devil by dabbling in the spiritual realm in this way. The 'client' is not required to do anything (apart from send the money) as they will be contacted by e-mail to be informed when they have completed the session. On one site I visited I noted that I was offered patience for $50 dollars, nothing unusual about that you might say. Then I read this, 'I will be doing a lot of earth healing during July and August so it may take a little longer than usual for me to fulfil your order. I appreciate your *patience*' (my italics). I would be tickled by the irony if it were not such a serious matter.

These sites have disclaimers that make them appear as if responsible people, who are genuinely concerned for the welfare of others, run them. They point out therefore (for fear of being pursued through legal channels I suggest) that their energy healing sessions are not intended to be medical or psychiatric treatment and/or a replacement for such treatment. But the reality is that such people have no regard for the well-being of their 'clients'. One day they will stand before the court of heaven and answer to the Almighty God for the activity from which they profit. These sites offer rather blatant counterfeits, but we should remember that people are genuinely seeking virtues such as the Holy Spirit gives to those whose lives are yielded to him, and desperate people will try desperate means!

Biblical patience

But now we leave that nefarious world behind as we try to come to a proper understanding of patience. The biblical meaning of 'patience' is deeper than its common usage today. It is the ability to endure delay, hardship and provocation. It is about perseverance and forbearance. Today we tend to think of patience as a quality that is admirable but not essential to good character. We have certainly been cut loose from our moorings on this issue because even a generation ago impatience was seen as a flaw in one's character. In Western society the sense of community is continuously disintegrating and being displaced with a ruthless individualism. People have become accustomed to the instant gratification of every desire and if their expectations are disappointed they are manifestly impatient. Patience, in a biblical sense, is not merely about biting your tongue when people and circumstances frustrate you. Again it has been anonymously stated that, 'patience is not passive: on the contrary it is active; it is concentrated strength.' This is important because we tend to think of patience as an attribute of character that we either have or do not have as if we have no control over the matter. Patience can be learned; it is not merely a trait that one is born with. Undoubtedly some people are more temperamentally suited to patience than others. It has been said, 'patience is a virtue, find it where you can, seldom in a woman, never in a man.' This may be generally true and I'm sure we could open up a fascinating discussion on such a topic but it is disturbing to hear Christians (whether they are male or female) say that they are not very patient. Sometimes it is said in such a way that one is meant to think that impatience is something to be proud of. It is as if the person is saying, 'I am a really dynamic get-the-job-done type of individual and I am unapologetic about my impatience with those who do not share my vision, work to my agenda and fall in with my pace.' Impatience is something to be ashamed of. Although some people are more inclined to be cool, calm and composed, patience is a quality that we should desire for ourselves. We ought to want it so that it may enhance all our relationships and the way we interact with others and ultimately bring glory to God. Perhaps the people of God could take their cue from the pastoral prayers of ministers who see the need for patience and the benefits it produces. The desire for patience can be stimulated from the pulpit. When God's servants strike this keynote in prayer others will see it as something to be pursued.

The testimony of patience

There are excellent opportunities to witness for Christ through patience. Patient husbands may win wives and patient wives may win husbands. Patient people stand out in the crowd. Paul instructs husbands to treat their wives patiently when he says, 'Husbands love your wives and do not be harsh with them' (Colossians 3:19). Every human relationship needs patience and perhaps none more so than marriage. Peter tells husbands to 'be considerate as you live with your wives and treat them with respect ... so that nothing will hinder your prayers' (1 Peter 3:7). The clear implication is that if husbands are inconsiderate and impatient with their wives their prayers may be ineffective. When Paul instructs wives to respect their husbands and submit to them he is calling on married women to exercise patience. The marriage relationship has a profound influence on the children of that relationship and therefore there is great responsibility to demonstrate patience. Children need to be disciplined patiently. Paul says 'Fathers, do not embitter your children, or they will become discouraged' (Colossians 3:21). Again in Ephesians he says 'Fathers do not exasperate your children ...' (6:4). Clearly we all have a responsibility (especially fathers) not only to be patient but to ensure that we do not cause others to become exasperated and impatient with us. Children are instructed in the same passage of Scripture to '... obey your parents in everything for this pleases the Lord' (Colossians 3:20). Obviously we need the grace of God to develop and display this fruit of the Spirit. May we exemplify this fruit as we walk in the Spirit!

We are to be patient with our families, with the family of God and with the human family. As we rub shoulders with others in the church and in the communities in which we live, in the workplace or at college we realise our need of patience. There is an assumption here that others may be a source of annoyance and provoke us to lose our patience. However, we need to think of ourselves as perhaps the cause of annoyance to others. Do we provoke others? Do we rouse people and incite them to anger? Do we stimulate impatience? Do we irritate others? In considering the possibility that we may be contributing to the impatience of others we are forced to look at our attitudes and actions. In doing this we may find that our own impatience is a provocation to others.

Patience stimulates patience

If we demonstrate patience it can diffuse potentially explosive situations and create a better climate for communication. As we have already stated biblical patience is about the ability to endure in circumstances of severe suffering. It is about riding the storms of provocation by perseverance. We are to be a people who continue steadfastly in trying conditions with a determination that is rooted in relationship to the one who endured the cross for our sakes. Patience is about forbearance which, in turn is about 'self-control'. Just as different fruit may have similar qualities so too 'patience' and 'self-control' have similarities. 'Self-control' is listed separately as fruit of the Holy Spirit and although it is related and has similar qualities it is best to consider it later.

If we are going to be patient people we will need to learn to overlook the faults and frailties of others. It is wise to have a sense of perspective that brings patience. Patience is an admirable and honourable quality. This is confirmed in Scripture: 'A man's wisdom gives him patience; it is to his glory to overlook an offence' (Proverbs' 19:11). Patience comes from wisdom and maturity and it lends a dignity to the one who exercises it. When we have that heavenly perspective where we can detach ourselves from the difficulties that would otherwise tend to arouse impatience, then it is not just a mark of honour to us but a glory to the Holy Spirit who produces such fruit in the life of the believer.

Praying for patience

Patience is greatly needed in this world in homes, (with husbands, wives, parents and children) churches and communities. The Christian is transformed in Christ and the transformed Christian personality ought to be patient in thought, word and deed. We have already said that patience is not merely passivity in challenging situations rather it is something active. The Holy Spirit desires to produce this fruit in the Christian life but in doing so the Spirit engages the emotions, intellect and will. This calls for our understanding of the importance and value of the concept of patience as well as our active co-operation in seeking to exercise it. We should, therefore, pray for patience for our fellow believers and ourselves. Paul writing to the Colossians says: 'For this reason, since the day we heard about you, we have not stopped praying for you and asking God to fill you with the knowledge of his will through all spiritual wisdom and understanding. And we pray this in order that you may live a life worthy of the Lord and may please him in every way: bearing fruit in every good work, growing in the knowledge of God, being strengthened with all power according to his glorious might so that you may have great endurance and patience' (Colossians 1:9–11). Exercising patience is part of what God expects from us. This is one means by which we live a life worthy of our calling in Christ.

Prayer and practice

We must remember that patience is a fruit of the Spirit. It is not, therefore, about digging deep within ourselves and seeking to tap inner resources! It is undoubtedly a rare and precious commodity in our post-modern world and many New-Age gurus would have us believe that it can be quarried from inner reserves. No doubt the human heart has potential for patience and we learn to practise it as we move from childhood to adulthood as part of our normal development. God has ordained that it should be so. Life teaches us patience as a coping strategy. Without it social interaction would be difficult if not impossible. But even people who are temperamentally inclined to patience have limits, and supernatural grace is needed to approximate anything of the patience of Christ. In terms of spiritual development we must learn that the kind of patience spoken about in Galatians 5 is qualitatively different. This is an exceptional spiritual quality that is deposited by God in rich seams in the converted human heart. It needs to be mined and processed through prayer and practice as we walk in the Spirit. This kind of supernatural patience bears testimony, not to our own abilities and determination but to God's power at work in us.

There may be occasions when we would be justified in reacting to provocation, and even though we could be proficient in putting people in their place, and yet we refrain from doing so. Godly patience produces thoughtful, measured and appropriate response. It can only come from a heart that has love, joy and peace in abundance. As such it is the outcome of a work that is already developed in the heart of the believer. It is the grace of God working itself through us in patience. The world marvels at it and God is glorified.

Examples of patience

Others who were called and commissioned by God exercised great patience and in doing this they were worthy ambassadors for God. James draws our attention to this: 'Brothers, as an example of patience in the face of suffering, take the prophets who spoke in the name of the Lord' (James 5:10). When the prophets were patient (they were not always patient; consider Jonah, for example) in their ministries they were demonstrating something of the character of God. Generally, however, the prophets were patient in situations of suffering. They endured hardship, ridicule, rejection and even death. We have already defined 'patience' in biblical terms as 'perseverance'. That tenacity and indefatigability is held in very high regard in Scripture. We see this well illustrated in the life of Job, for example. Thus James, having drawn our attention to the example of the patience of the prophets, goes on to say: 'As you know, we consider blessed those who have persevered. You have heard of Job's perseverance and have seen what the Lord finally brought about. The Lord is full of compassion and mercy' (James 5:11).

Purpose in patience

The Lord wants to accomplish his purposes through our patience. Even the world recognises something exceptional and extraordinary in 'the patience of Job'. His perspective was shaped by confidence that God was in control. Patience is established on a serenity that comes from being entirely satisfied with God's will and pleasure. As Ezekiel Hopkins said 'patience is the ballast of the soul that will keep it from rolling and tumbling in the greatest storms'. Thus the example of the prophets and the exemplary life of Job are recorded in Scripture not merely that we might comprehend that they were patient. Rather these things are recorded so that we might learn from the instruction inherent in their telling. Thus Paul tells the Romans, 'For everything that was written in the past was written to teach us, so that through endurance and the encouragement of the Scriptures we might have hope' (Romans 15:4). When we are in situations that sorely test our patience we may rest in the knowledge that we are in his will and be encouraged that he is at work in us as he was in the prophets and patriarchs of old. We may become impatient when we see unplanned events interrupting our day. But those interruptions are frequently God's way of teaching us about right responses.

Perfect Patience

Our patience is challenged on every front. Parents have to exercise patience with children (and vice-versa). Wives have to exercise patience with husbands (and vice-versa). Employers have to exercise patience with employees (and vice-versa) and so on in all the myriad of human relationships. The disciple of Christ is called to model the Master and he is the supreme example of all the fruit of the Spirit, including patience. When we were at enmity with God he did not destroy us. If our God were not patient nobody would be saved from his wrath. If God were prone to furious outbursts of temper none of us would be spared. We have provoked him with our rebelliousness and wrongdoing but he has been infinitely patient. Let us recall the incident on the night of his arrest when Jesus showed great restraint. Do you remember how Peter drew his sword and struck the servant of the High Priest cutting off his ear? Then Jesus spoke to him: '"Put your sword back in its place," Jesus said to him, "for all who draw the sword will die by the sword. Do you think I cannot call on my Father, and he will at once put at my disposal more than twelve legions of angels? But how then would the Scriptures be fulfilled that say it must happen in this way?"' (Matthew 26:52–54). This is a supreme example of patience rooted in confidence that the will of God is being fulfilled and we do well to take note of it. May we have confidence in the sovereign will of God when our patience is tested!

Recall too that occasion when Christ hung on the cross and was humiliated and taunted. He exercised astonishing patience. He could have called on the angels of heaven to take him down from the cross and avenge his tormentors. Yet he spoke to his Father in heaven and said: 'Father, forgive them, for they do not know what they are doing' (Luke 23:34). God is patient! We know this experientially but we are also told in Scripture that this is so. Peter says '... He is patient with you' (2 Peter 3:9). Scripture also speaks of God as 'slow to anger' (*árék 'appayim*) (See, for example, Exodus 34:6; Numbers 14:18; Nehemiah 9:17; Psalm 86:15; Psalm 103:8; Psalm 145:8; Joel 2:13; Jonah 4:2; Nahum 1:3). This, as we have seen, is the true meaning of *patience*. The Master is our model. He was patient with the disciples who were slow and weak and cowardly. He was patient with his persecutors. He calls us to be like him and exercise patience. God's patience is perfect. Paul writing to the Romans speaks to them about the '... riches of his kindness, tolerance and patience ...' (Romans 2:4).

Patience is an attribute of God's character. The Christian is ever conscious of God's patience and ever grateful to be beneficiaries of that perfect distinguishing mark of grace. Paul was intensely aware of the fact that he deserved the wrath of God but he was equally greatly mindful of God's patience as a facet of grace. Thus he wrote to Timothy: 'But for that very reason I was shown mercy so that in me, the worst of sinners, Christ Jesus might display his unlimited patience as an example for those who would believe on him and receive eternal life' (1 Timothy 1:16). God's patience is purposeful in that it serves the eternal agenda of salvation and brings glory to his name! Each one of us is a living example of God's perfect and purposeful patience. We see that patience perfectly illustrated in the life of Christ, in his words and deeds, especially at Calvary! Grace is not just

God's unmerited favour to undeserving sinners rather it is God's unmerited favour to hell-deserving sinners!

Modelling the master

The example par-excellence of patience is Jesus. The character of God is displayed in Christ and we are called to consider him as our role model. The writer to the Hebrews exhorts the believer to put Christ in the centre of the frame, to focus on him. Thus we read: 'Therefore, since we are surrounded by such a great cloud of witnesses, let us throw off everything that hinders and the sin that so easily entangles, and let us run with perseverance the race marked out for us. Let us fix our eyes on Jesus, the author and perfecter of our faith, who for the joy set before him endured the cross, scorning its shame, and sat down at the right hand of the throne of God. Consider him who endured such opposition from sinful men, so that you will not grow weary and lose heart' (Hebrews 12:1–3). The Christian life is a race that demands a patient and persevering approach. The one who quickened our hearts with faith is at work to perfect that faith through a patient lifestyle. James too, emphasises this when he encourages the saints to 'Consider it pure joy, my brothers, whenever you face trials of many kinds, because you know that the testing of your faith develops perseverance. Perseverance must finish its work so that you may be mature and complete, not lacking anything' (James 1:2–4). God is at work in the lives of believers shaping and perfecting so that those who are his may bear fruit for his glory.

If God had lost patience with mankind where would we be? We would be without hope, hurtling through time into eternity and hell. Consider how patient he was when he was falsely accused, tried, beaten, mocked, humiliated and crucified. He is our model and our motivation.

Devotional distinctiveness

We talk much about the *doctrinal* distinctiveness that sets us apart from the heresies of false religion but here in the fruit of the Spirit (including 'patience') is *devotional* distinctiveness that identifies us as true disciples of Christ! Consider the exhortation of Paul, 'Therefore, as God's chosen people, holy and dearly loved, clothe yourselves with compassion, kindness, humility, gentleness and patience' (Colossians 3:12). Each day we clothe our bodies in preparation for the day ahead and here Paul instructs us to put on 'patience' amongst other things. Just as clothing our physical bodies demands our active participation in the selection of suitable clothing and the act of dressing so in the spiritual realm we need to select 'patience' as a garment befitting the day and actively put it on. Patience is a garment of glory supplied by God through the fruit of the indwelling Spirit. Patience is a mark of character; God's character. He is moulding our characters to be more like him. That is what godliness is. That is what Christ-likeness is. That ongoing process of sanctification has commenced and will continue until it is complete in Christ. Thus Paul could tell the Philippians that he was, and they too may be, 'confident of this, that he who began a good work in you will carry it on to completion until the day of Christ Jesus' (Philippians 1:6). We can say this with Paul because like him we can proclaim that we too know the one to whom we have entrusted our lives, 'I know whom I have believed, and am convinced that he is able to guard what I have entrusted to him for that day' (2 Timothy 1:12).

Times of trial when patience is tested are ultimately beneficial because they work toward perfecting Christian character. Knowing this is a wonderful consolation. As Paul said to the Romans '... we also rejoice in our sufferings, because we know that suffering produces perseverance; perseverance, character ...' (Romans 5: 3–4).

Remembering that we are redeemed and forgiven much should help us to be patient with each other. We must learn to forgive like Christ forgave. He forgave extravagantly. We must learn to be patient with one another for Christ's sake.

Pastoral preaching
Finally it must be said that those who are called to preach the Word must do so with patience. Just as Jesus was patient with his disciples so the preacher needs to be patient in the way he communicates divine truth. Our preaching should have this pastoral element. This is a sacred trust and its duties must be carried out as God desires. Thus Paul instructs Timothy to 'Preach the Word; be prepared in season and out of season; correct, rebuke and encourage—with great patience and careful instruction.' (2 Timothy 4: 2).

The preacher is not just to fulfil the task of explaining God's Word but he is to do so in a manner that is Christ-like, with 'great patience'.

Problems produce patience

God may permit problems to enter our lives in order to discipline and lovingly develop our characters. It is in such times, as we wait patiently on God, that we find direction from him. Waiting for guidance may be very difficult but in such times we go deeper in self-examination and grow more dependent on the counsel of his Word, the affirmation of other mature Christians, the mind of the church and the providential leading of God. As we look to Jesus for guidance, in patient and persevering prayer, we do so knowing that his timing is perfect and his placements are just right. We learn to trust him patiently because being impatient with God comes from a failure of faith, a failure to appreciate the sovereignty of God and a failure to accept his providential care. However, it is easy to be philosophical about biblical characters that savoured the sovereignty of God and patiently proved his providence. A man such as Joseph inspires us and teaches us much, but the application of these truths is not learned fully in abstract. Rather they are acquired in the crucible of experience. It is often in difficult times that our theology is tested, and so it is in the problems of life that our walk in the Spirit produces the fruit of patience. We are not born fully-grown in the physical realm, so too in the spiritual realm there is a period of growth. We should remember this when considering the fruit of the Spirit because essentially we are talking about growth in grace.

God wants us to deal with our disappointments and difficulties in a way that is honouring to him and not in a manner that brings the faith we profess into disrepute. Are we patient fathers, patient mothers, patient children, patient work colleagues, patient neighbours and patient drivers? In a world that is becoming increasingly congested with cars, delays and gridlock are a frequent reality for many and incidents of road rage are on the increase. It may be difficult to keep our composure and remain patient in today's traffic in many cities, but it cannot be right that the Christian should be aggressive like many other road users. Being patient is something we chose. We learn patterns of behaviour by frequently choosing certain responses. If we are impatient then it is because we have opted for the wrong kind of responses and we need to unlearn this as a necessary first step toward learning patience.

Righteous reputation

Christians should have a reputation for patience. Proverbs tells us that 'A hot-tempered man stirs up dissension, but a patient man calms a quarrel' (15:18). We know this makes perfect sense. The Christian should be the one in the community quelling racial hatred at the residents committee meeting, mediating in situations where conflict resolution is needed and so on. Our names should be the names that spring to mind when cool-headed thinking is required. Unfortunately many of us have the opposite reputation and we are thought to be frenzied fanatics. Some of this reputation may be undeserved but perhaps we have not always done all that we could in legitimate protests to present our point of view patiently! Paul instructs us to 'be patient with everyone' (1 Thessalonians 5:14). This involves far more than pretending to be patient in the Sunday services! Your patience might just be the catalyst that produces what the Spirit desires to accomplish in your church. Your patience might be like a stone dropped in the centre of a lake, the ripples spread in ever-widening circles to the shore. Patience in our homes will extend to our churches. Patience in our churches will spread to our communities. Patience in our communities may, in time, reach other parts of the country and possibly the effect will eventually be felt even in the most distant places. The potential of patience is enormous.

Hopeful and helpful

Being patient may mean that we have to learn to change our goals and expectations. This is not about compromising our integrity or settling for inefficiency and poor standards. Rather this is about perspective. We need to allow ourselves and others more time and space to develop. We need to focus on what has been achieved and not just on what still needs to be done. Impatience condemns and focuses on faults and failings whereas patience finds a way forward because it is hopeful and helpful in times when hope and help is most needed. If we expect perfection all around us we will be miserable, frustrated and disappointed. In reality we become impatient when we feel our rights have been transgressed and we lash out in defence.

Or we become impatient when somebody does not meet our expectations. Greater humility and spiritual reorientation will enable us to be patient people. Patience is sustained in the knowledge that God is sovereign and in control of the details of our lives. We ought not to want a life that is free from problems, rather to know patience in the midst of difficulties. This is faith because it says, '… we know that in all things God works for the good of those who love him …' (Romans 8:28). Real patience comes from a real relationship with Jesus.

The kind of patience that we find listed as fruit of the Spirit comes from God and has been demonstrated by countless numbers of Christians in times of opposition and oppression. This reflects something of the nature of God. He has been patient in his dealings with a sinful and rebellious human race that is fully deserving of his wrath. How often he pleaded with Jerusalem (Mark 12:1–11). How often he restored a rebellious Israel (Hosea 11:8–9). How graciously he spared Nineveh. We live in a time when there is still a window of opportunity for repentance until the return of the Lord. As we await the Lord's Second Coming each day is a day of grace in a prolonged age of patience.

Let us be patient in times of trial, affliction and chastisement for the cause of the gospel. Patience is about enduring and persevering in confident hope of the sovereignty and providence of God. Occasions which demand patience are opportunities for the perfection of Christian character. In knowing 'the patience of Christ' (2 Thessalonians 3:5) we are challenged to be patient in our suffering as he was in his. Christ had that quality of character whereby he exercised restraint in the face of great provocation. He does not hastily retaliate or promptly punish. Christ was fully aware that he was not a victim of circumstances that were beyond the control of God. He was in control and willingly submitted to his divinely appointed destiny. We must see that our lives are in his care. In this way we rest patiently in the eternal outcome.

Kindness

'But the fruit of the Spirit is … kindness …'

At a wedding reception some time ago I was seated beside a lady who had contracted polio in childhood and she was lame in both feet. She used two walking canes and hobbled into her seat. She had recently come to faith in Christ and she was as radiant as the bride. My thoughts were turned to Mephibosheth.

In Old Testament times when a king died and a new family came to power it was common for the new king to seek out and destroy any remaining members of the previous king's family. In this way his throne and dynasty would be secured. In 2 Samuel 9:1–13 we read about Mephibosheth. After Saul died David became king and he began to look for any surviving members of Saul's family. He was informed that Saul had a grandson named Mephibosheth. So Mephibosheth was summoned to David's palace. Imagine how fearful he must have felt. But David did not intend to kill him; instead he was going to show him kindness: 'So Mephibosheth ate at David's table like one of the king's sons' (v. 11b). David showed kindness to him and our God has shown unlimited and unfailing kindness to us.

A place at the top table

David's treatment of an undeserving member of Saul's family reminds us of how God treats us: 'with everlasting kindness I will have compassion on you' (Isaiah 54:8). This kindness to Mephibosheth serves to illustrate the kindness and love of God to fallen man, namely, us! We were brought low, lamed and impoverished by the fall of Adam. We were convicted of rebellion against God and should have been under the sentence of rejection from him. What a privileged position Mephibosheth was given, to have the provision, protection and presence of the king. He didn't spurn that invitation but accepted it and he was given a place of privilege at the banqueting table, something akin to being seated at the top table at a wedding reception: 'As for Mephibosheth' said the king, 'he shall eat at my table like one of the king's sons' (v. 11, NKJV).

The kindness of salvation

Here is a striking picture of salvation by grace that shows us something of kindness. Grace is unmerited favour to the undeserving, kindness to a helpless one. Paul sums it up in Ephesians 2:1, 4–7 (NKJV) 'And you he made alive, who were dead in trespasses and sins, but God, who is rich in mercy, because of his great love with which he loved us, even when we were dead in trespasses, made us alive together with Christ (by grace you have been saved), and raised us up together, and made us sit together in the heavenly places in Christ Jesus, that in the ages to come he might show the exceeding riches of his grace in his kindness toward us in Christ Jesus.'

The kindness of adoption

Every Christian has the right to be called a child of God: 'For you are all sons of God through faith in Christ Jesus' (Galatians 3:26, NKJV). This is as true for us as it was for the Galatians. Mephibosheth was sought out and found in a distant place called Lo Debar, far from the family estate and David's court. He was crippled in both feet, the result of a tragic fall. Here is a picture of all of humanity! With us too God took the initiative, sought us out and found us in a distant place far from his kingdom. The Son of God enquired after a degenerate people, who didn't enquire after him. To those who humble and commit themselves before him as Mephibosheth did before David he restores the forfeited inheritance. He takes them into communion with himself and sets them at his banqueting table and spreads a feast of the dainties of heaven before them. This is what God the Father has done for us and it is greater than what David did for Mephibosheth because we have been adopted with full inheritance rights! 'But when the fullness of the time had come, God sent forth his Son, born of a woman, born under the law, to redeem those who were under the law, that we might receive the adoption as sons. And because you are sons, God has sent forth the Spirit of his Son into your hearts, crying out, "'Abba, Father!" Therefore you are no longer a slave but a son, and if a son, then an heir of God through Christ' (Galatians 4:4–7, NKJV).

Kindness creates confidence

In the Old Testament the idea of God's holiness was the pre-eminent thought. The keynote of that concept of God is found in Isaiah 6:3 'Holy, holy, holy, is the Lord Almighty' Holiness underscores God's distinctive character and the distance between our piety and his purity. The New Testament reflects a shift in emphasis. God is still the holy being that he always was, but instead of relating to us as a king to his subjects he relates to us as a father to his children. What wonderful kindness! Under the old covenant God could be approached cautiously through the mediation of the priesthood. There were specific regulations that had to be observed. Whereas Moses was commanded to take off his shoes we are invited to 'approach God with freedom and confidence' (Ephesians 3:12).

We have been justified but we are not just wards of that heavenly court. We have been adopted into the family of God. Our standing with God is not only based on the satisfaction of legal requirements but it is also based on a loving relationship. We are neither slaves nor servants, though we offer service, and we are not merely subjects of a king. We are children! Let us, therefore accept the invitation of the writer to the Hebrews '... Since we have confidence to enter the Most Holy Place ... let us draw near to God with a sincere heart, in full assurance of faith' (Hebrews 10: 19ff). We feel comfortable in the presence of kind people.

We, like Mephibosheth, were crippled and condemned to live in a distant and barren place. But we have been accepted and restored in Christ. Indeed God has been kind to us!

This should stir our souls to sing:

'Where shall my wandering soul begin?
O how shall I the goodness tell
Father which thou to me has showed?
That I a child of wrath and hell,
I should be called a child of God' (Charles Wesley).

This is the soul-stirring anthem of the citizens of heaven.

Kindness kindles responsibility

Adoption has great privileges and great responsibilities. In the physical realm children bear a certain likeness to their fathers. Their voices, mannerisms, gestures, posture and so on. In the spiritual realm there ought to be something about us that is distinctively Christ-like, especially our attitudes and actions. Surely we are to be kind people. There is such a great need for kindness in this cold world! Healthy and happy families care for each other and help each other. So too in the spiritual realm we must support and love each other in the kindness of the Holy Spirit. Families have reputations that are guarded jealously. Any one member can bring dishonour on the family. So let us make every effort to avoid bringing God's family into disrepute, especially by being unkind. Let us, who have experienced the kindness of God exhibit that kindness as a fruit of the Spirit in our lives!

Kind provision

In 2 Samuel 9 the kindness of David to Mephibosheth is recorded. David sent an invitation and made kind provision. God has done no less for us. He is the great benefactor of love, forgiveness and acceptance and we are the beneficiaries. Heirs in the world may be disinherited. A worldly inheritance is subject to devaluation but our inheritance is not subject to decay or devaluation and we will never be disinherited. As children of God we have privileges and status according to the position of the father who is 'King of Kings'!

David says that he wishes to show kindness 'for Jonathan's sake'. He was keeping a covenant promise he made with Jonathan. God has made a covenant promise to all those who are in Christ and if a sinner, like David, could fulfil his promise, do you think God will fail to fulfil his? God promises eternal and abundant life. He promises constant companionship that is personal and perpetual (Hebrews 3:5). Surely we derive courage and contentment from this.

Continuing kindness

In verse 3 David refers to the kindness of God, 'Is there not still someone of the house of Saul, to whom I may show the kindness of God? (NKJV)' All the land and all the possessions of Saul were restored to Mephibosheth. In Christ there is restoration and blessing, 'you shall eat bread at my table continually' (v. 7) and it is forever! Grace saves and sustains 'And I give them eternal life, and they shall never perish; neither shall anyone snatch them out of my hand … My Father, who has given them to me, is greater than all; and no one is able to snatch them out of my Father's hand' (John 10:28–29, NKJV).

Consider the scope of this kindness. Mephibosheth always ate at the king's table; it was not a temporary arrangement. He had fixed appointments in the authority of the king! When we come together in fellowship it is because we have fixed appointments in the authority of the king. The Lord's Table is the symbol of that banquet of grace. 'How great is the love the Father has lavished on us, that we should be called children of God! And that is what we are!' (1 John 3:1).

In verse 7 David says to Mephibosheth 'do not fear'; Jesus said, 'Let not your heart be troubled' (John 14:1, NKJV). These are kind and inviting words. God draws us to himself and dispels our fears with kind reassuring words. Grace gives a place of privilege to its recipients, namely us! 'Blessed be the God and Father of our Lord Jesus Christ, who has blessed us with every spiritual blessing in the heavenly places in Christ, just as he chose us in him before the foundation of the world, that we should be holy and without blame before him in love, having predestined us to adoption as sons by Jesus Christ to himself, according to the good pleasure of his will, to the praise of the glory of his grace, by which he has made us accepted in the Beloved' (Ephesians 1:3–6, NKJV). God, in kindness, accepts us because we belong to him! We were bought with his precious blood and we are his treasured possession. We should relish our adoption and revel in its kindness and eternal implications for us: '"As for Mephibosheth," said the king, "he shall eat at my table like one of the king's sons"' (v. 11, NKJV). We, too, are invited to sit with him at the top table at that great banquet that awaits the redeemed. This is overwhelming kindness! Let us savour our status as sons!

There we leave the story of David and Mephibosheth, one of the greatest illustrations of kindness in Scripture in that it illustrates the kindness of God. As beneficiaries of such abundant kindness we are now in a position to become benefactors of that grace. In other words we can show kindness to others because we have experienced great kindness and know the power of kindness in demonstrating the love of God.

Reflecting God's kindness

Generally we speak of a kind person as someone who shares something of what they have. The greatest thing that we possess is knowledge of God's grace. We must strive to share this great gospel with those who need to know the kindness of God. One does not have to be very rich materially to share money and be generous in other ways. Acts of kindness have many manifestations. Kindness tells us something about who a person is. In other words *how* kind we are shows *what* kind we are! What kind of person are you? As Christians we cherish the noble name of Christ and we should also bear the benevolent nature of Christ! In this we are merely being true to kind. We are being true to our new nature and to God's nature. This is what the fruit of the Spirit is, being true to the nature of God. Apple trees bear apples. Christians bear the fruit of the Spirit. In being generous we reflect something of the generosity of God. When God gave he spared nothing for he gave his only Son. When God gives he does so with extravagance. His giving is magnanimous and open-handed. Jonathan appealed to David for 'kindness like that of the Lord' (see 1 Samuel 20:14–15). Most people today have that expectation of Christians. That is why they are able to identify hypocrisy so easily. As J.C. Ryle said, 'kindness is a grace that all can understand'. If we are not very kind we are not very Christian.

Contradicting Christ's kindness

The opposite of kindness is meanness, harshness, cruelty and severity. The Christian who is like that is a disgrace, not just to himself but also and especially to God! If we are small-minded, shabby, malicious and ill tempered we should wonder, as others undoubtedly do, if we are Christians at all! When we consider the context in which Paul lists the fruit of the Spirit we see that he is talking about qualities that distinguish the believer in his new life from features of his old life, outside Christ. The verses immediately preceding those listing the fruit of the Spirit identify the characteristics of life in the flesh: 'hatred, discord, jealousy, fits of rage, selfish ambition, dissensions, factions and envy' (Galatians 5:20–21). If these are the hallmarks of those outside Christ, and if they are still evident in the lives of those who claim to be followers of Christ, then there is legitimate warrant to be concerned that such people do not actually belong to Jesus. No amount of theological knowledge, church attendance, public prayer, preaching or use of Christian terminology will mask a deficiency in kindness. As Frederick W. Faber said, 'kindness has converted more sinners than zeal, eloquence or learning.' Kindness is a sharp instrument in God's hands and if we want to be instrumental in the purposes of God in his kingdom then we must be characterised by kindness.

Unworthy recipients

If we bestow kindness on those who have earned it or are worthy of it then we are not behaving like God and therefore not truly Christ-like. Kindness begins with a consciousness in our own experience that we are unworthy of blessing. Thus in Jacob's prayer we read, 'I am unworthy of all the kindness … you have shown your servant' (Genesis 32:10). As we go on in the Christian life we become ever more aware that God is always kind to us. Even though we may find ourselves in difficult circumstances, God's kindness is at work for our good and his glory. Thus Scripture tells us of Joseph that, 'while Joseph was there in the prison, the LORD was with him; he showed him kindness and granted him favour in the eyes of the prison warder' (Genesis 39:20–21).

Other Illustrations

We have looked at the relationship between David and Mephibosheth as a splendid illustration of the kindness of God. We could equally well have examined the story of Ruth. In the book of Ruth we see great kindness. There we read of the kindness of Ruth to Naomi and also of the kindness of Boaz to Ruth. In these also we see pictures of God's kindness to us and they thrill our souls and stimulate us to demonstrate that kindness to others.

Generating kindness

Another very interesting dimension to kindness is the fact that it often generates a reciprocal response. In Scripture we sometimes see how kindness begets kindness. Thus we read in 2 Samuel 2: 'When David was

Kindness

told that it was the men of Jabesh Gilead who had buried Saul, he sent messengers to the men of Jabesh Gilead to say to them, 'The LORD bless you for showing this kindness to Saul your master by burying him. May the LORD now show you kindness and faithfulness, and I too will show you the same favour because you have done this' (vs. 4–6). Another passage of Scripture that illustrates how kindness begets kindness is 1 Kings 2:7, 'But show kindness to the sons of Barzillai of Gilead and let them be among those who eat at your table. They stood by me when I fled from your brother Absalom.' Kindness is conceived in love and expressed in loyalty. Little acts of kindness can salvage relationships that are in danger of disintegrating. My wife remembers a day in primary school when she was upset by the cruel and unfair treatment of a teacher. Another teacher was moved to pity and gave her very own handkerchief to the sobbing child. My wife tells me it smelled of perfume and had the kind teacher's initials embroidered on it. Even though it was a generation ago and may seem like a simple and insignificant gesture of kindness it is still remembered with gratitude and fondness. It tells us something of what that person was really like. We respond well to kindness.

Something to sing about

In David's Song he acknowledges the kindness of God, 'He gives his king great victories; he shows unfailing kindness to his anointed, to David and his descendants for ever' (2 Samuel 22:51). Surely that kindness is worth singing about. It is a glorious theme, an anthem of the citizens of heaven. As the hymn writer put it:

For the love of God is broader
Than the measures of man's mind;
And the heart of the Eternal
Is most wonderfully kind.[1]

Let us acknowledge the kindness of God.

Kindness in affliction

Ezra acknowledged God's deliverance of a wayward people from bondage to be an act of kindness: 'Though we are slaves, our God has not deserted us in our bondage. He has shown us kindness in the sight of the kings of Persia' (Ezra 9:9). Even in less than ideal circumstances the people of God can readily acknowledge the kindness of God. We all too readily see the kindness of God in the favourable situations of our lives, but the challenge is to confess the kindness of God even in great affliction. In spite of great calamity Job could say, 'You gave me life and showed me kindness, and in your providence watched over my spirit' (Job 10:12). From my experience as a pastor I can say that the most wonderful testimony to the grace of God is to hear a child of God who has suffered much acknowledge the kindness of God in his affliction. The bereaved and broken-hearted who attest to the kindness of God are drenched in the fragrance of Jesus. God sometimes allows great sorrow to be entrusted to those who are strong enough (by his grace) to honour him.

God delights in kindness

The Lord delights in kindness and calls on us to recognise this side of his nature, 'Let him who boasts boast about this: that he understands and knows me, that I am the LORD, who exercises kindness, justice and righteousness on earth, for in these I delight' (Jeremiah 9:24). When you were a child did you ever boast about your father? This is what God wants us to be like; children who are proud of our Father's character and who feel that their glory is only in him. Our God is wonderfully kind! Meditate on this and treasure it in your heart.

God's common grace to humanity is proclaimed by Barnabas and Paul (as the kindness of God) to the people in Lystra: 'Yet he has not left himself without testimony: He has shown kindness by giving you rain from heaven and crops in their seasons; he provides you with plenty of food and fills your hearts with joy' (Acts 14:17). Yet God's kindness goes largely unacknowledged in the world. The Christian, therefore, ought to bear witness to it and be channels of that grace to others. One simple way of showing kindness is to offer hospitality. It is all too easy to be hospitable to your friends and those who are popular in the church. What about the large family who are seldom or never offered hospitality because it would be too much trouble or expense? Spare a thought for the socially awkward person who is off the hospitality list. Clearly one can observe hospitality rituals and still not be kind. This kind of self-deception may be regularly practised among Christians.

A record of kindness

The Maltese are identified in Scripture for their kindness because they were genuinely hospitable to Paul and the many others who were shipwrecked with him on the Island of Malta. 'Once safely on shore, we found out that the island was called Malta. The islanders showed us unusual kindness. They built a fire and welcomed us all because it was raining and cold' (Acts 28:1–2). They met the needs of desperate people; prisoners without possessions. There would hardly be a chance of reciprocal hospitality but that did not matter. We can still look outside the household of faith and see wonderful examples of kindness in our needy world. But let us not be put to shame by being outshone in acts of magnanimous kindness.

The future dimension

There is more than just a present dimension to the kindness of God; there is also a future aspect to that dispensation of his love. Thus Paul says to the Ephesians: 'And God raised us up with Christ and seated us with him in the heavenly realms in Christ Jesus, in order that in the coming ages he might show the incomparable riches of his grace, expressed in his kindness to us in Christ Jesus' (2:6–7). We will have all eternity to comprehend and enjoy the 'incomparable riches of his grace, expressed in his kindness to us in Christ Jesus.' For within the limitations of our mortality we cannot possibly plumb the depths of such kindness.

Getting dressed

With regard to the practical outworking of kindness as fruit of the Spirit we should take heed of Paul's instruction to the Colossians to clothe themselves with kindness: 'Therefore, as God's chosen people, holy and dearly loved, clothe yourselves with compassion, kindness, humility, gentleness and patience' (Colossians 3:12). Consider this for a moment. Clothes are external and evident things that we consciously put on our bodies each day. They are what people immediately see when they look at us. They distinguish us from others so that we may speak of the man in the blue shirt with the red tie. We must consciously exhibit kindness. It is not something that will just automatically happen without an effort on our part. Kindness, together with the other fruit of the Spirit will distinguish us from others and identify us as belonging to Christ. The garments Christ provides are like a school uniform that identifies us as his disciples. Nevertheless the analogy is not perfect insofar as clothes are merely external to the body whereas the fruit of the Spirit is an outward appearance rooted in a new, organic inner nature. There are clothes that express national identity, ethnic belonging and religious affiliation that might better connect the inner reality being expressed in the outward garments.

Kindness incarnate

But there we leave that analogy and move on to a very interesting verse in Titus that tells us that kindness is a quality of God's character that is so connected to who he is that it is difficult to tell 'the dancer from the dance' so to speak. 'But when the kindness and love of God our Saviour appeared' (Titus 3:4). Christ is kindness incarnate! His miracles were acts of kindness. His encounter with the woman taken in adultery was an act of kindness. The gospels are rich in accounts of his kindness to others: the undeserving, outsiders, the rejected and so on. We are to be like him! We need to work at it, to try to perfect it. Acts of kindness count for something in God's estimation.

Love is kind

Thus kindness is recorded in the New Testament lists of what we are to achieve and what God wants us to be. As an example, let us take inventory from the following list in Peter's second epistle where he says: 'For this very reason, make every effort to add to your faith goodness; and to goodness, knowledge; and to knowledge, self-control; and to self-control, perseverance; and to perseverance, godliness; and to godliness, brotherly kindness; and to brotherly kindness, love' (1:5–7). Kindness is caring about the other person's needs. It is a practical demonstration of love. In that great passage on love Paul tells us that, 'love is kind' (1 Corinthians 13:4). The sinful nature of people's hearts makes them selfish and unkind.

Kindness undervalued

Frequently in television programmes, kind people are surrounded by cynical people who are frequently sarcastic and sometimes cruel. It is a telling comment on our society that the kind person is often portrayed as an oddball. They dress in ways that are old-fashioned and their behaviour is presented as quirky. The message seems to be that it is not cool to be kind!

The challenge

We have seen kindness in the Scriptures and explored the idea that God's character is kind. We have touched on several exhortations for us to be kind. We know that it is godly and good advice. We accept that kindness is evidence of spiritual maturity. What remains for us now is to go and be kind! May there be kindness in our thoughts and speech. Let us remember that speech is a test of true Christianity (James) because it reveals what is inside the heart. Let us remember that harsh words wound people and damage relationships and divide churches. On the other hand kind words from believers come from the influence of the Holy Spirit. Let us, therefore speak words of comfort and encouragement to build up rather than tear down.

We must not become so preoccupied with other things, even things that are good and right, that we have no time to be kind to others. Many people have been so committed to some noble cause that they have neglected to be kind to those nearest to them. Task oriented people may achieve much but at what cost? Process oriented people are more aware and concerned about what is happening in the process as they move toward their goal. Christ was committed to the greatest possible cause and yet he took time to be kind to others. He fulfilled his mission in a manner that showed great consideration for the needs of others. The gospels are full of accounts of Jesus taking time to be kind. He was not too busy in ministry to listen and help. Some high profile men in ministry today would do well to model themselves on him rather than the unapproachable and even unreachable top executive! Let us meditate on Christ as we read the gospels and may the personality of the Saviour permeate our souls and percolate through to others in our sphere of influence.

When we consider kindness there is a challenge for us to be kind with our material substance. Kindness is costly. In this we have the example of the early church where the believers sold their possessions and gave to those who had need. In this practical way of caring for one another we see that kindness is another dimension of love. Kindness is love expressed in little or large acts and in showing kindness to others we are demonstrating the love of God for his glory. The kindness of God should produce a faith that is kind and compassionate not the hyper-righteous hypocrisy that seems to characterise religion without grace. Our God is a tender God. He is the Good Shepherd who cares and tends his sheep. In Isaiah we read those beautiful words, 'He tends his flock like a shepherd: He gathers the lambs in his arms and carries them close to his heart; he gently leads those that have young' (40:11). We must not be hard-hearted, strict and legalistic because that conveys a false impression of God to others and it is also idolatrous! For God is not like that and if we worship such a 'god' we are not worshipping the one true God. God is kind. He declares this in Jeremiah, 'I am the LORD, who exercises kindness' (9:24). God's kindness is intended to lead sinners to repentance (Romans 2:4). John tells us that 'God is love' (1 John 4:8) and let us remind ourselves that Paul tells us, in 1 Corinthians, that one of the qualities of love is kindness (13:4).

We live in a world where kindness may be exploited and this may have the effect of causing us to repress urges to be kind. Ultimately this will make us unkind and, therefore, unlike Christ. I recently saw a bumper sticker that said, 'commit random acts of kindness.' Perhaps we would all do well to make this slogan a reality in the lives of those around us!

Central to true religion

Jesus told us that kindness is central to true religion. Let us consider the powerful parable of the Good Samaritan (Luke 10:30–35). It is, in spite of our familiarity with it, a story that still has a tremendous impact today. Jesus is defining and describing true neighbourliness in this parable. The Word of God tells us to 'love your neighbour' (Leviticus 19:18; Matthew 5:43; Matthew 19:19; Matthew 22:39; Mark 12:31; Mark 12:33; Luke 10:27; Romans 13:9; Galatians 5:14; James 2:8). Again it bears repeating that Paul tells us that 'love is kind' (1 Corinthians 13:4). We are not stretching the point therefore when we say that this Samaritan loved his neighbour and expressed that real love in genuine, practical kindness. In this he was like Christ who was not indifferent to the misery of others. Needy people were not merely an obstacle to his plans. Jesus was neither unaware nor unconcerned about the needs of others.

In this parable a priest passed by possibly because he was aware that if he touched a dead person he would be rendered unclean and thereby unable to perform his religious duties in the Temple (Numbers 19:11). He may not have been sure if the man was alive. It was a risk he was not prepared to take. Then a Levite passed. We know that bandits used that road to rob people. Maybe the Levite speculated that the man lying on the ground was part of a gang of robbers and that the scene was created to trap whoever might stop to give assistance. In this we are speculating as to the possible reasons why two religious men failed to show basic human kindness. We are not sure why they behaved as they did and we are merely making a reasonable effort to understand what possible reason(s) they may have had for their disreputable behaviour. Their avoidance was most likely not exceptional. They probably encountered this sort of thing regularly and habitually ignored the plight of others. Sadly there seems to be a connection between what they believed and how they behaved. We should be careful to ensure that our religion is characterised by a real relationship with God rather than merely adhering to ritualistic regulations.

The right instinct
In marked contrast a Samaritan acted with kindness. He was obviously a kind person who was acting in character. The instinct of the two religious men was self-protection whereas the instinct of the Samaritan was the need of the one who had been robbed and beaten. How blind and indifferent we can become to the terrible needs of those around us. We can become indifferent to the harrowing circumstances of the destitute and homeless. We can be put to shame by the secular agencies that act compassionately to provide for their needs. Does it seem to the world that we are more concerned with religious ceremony than with practical kindness? Do we,

metaphorically, or even literally, cross to the other side of the road to avoid having to face the challenge to our kindness that is presented in the needs of others? The Good Samaritan went beyond compassionate feelings and demonstrated actual kindness. Jesus told this parable to people who were aware that such incidents frequently occurred on the road from Jerusalem to Jericho. We read it and hear it today in a world where there are many uncomfortable parallels. Will we avoid opportunities to show kindness or will we take the risk and get involved? Many Christian young people today wear the bracelet with the letters W.W.J.D? This stands for 'What Would Jesus Do?' We need be in no doubt about what Jesus would do, and what he would want us to do. Our reasons for not getting involved may be reasonable and even religious but they are really just excuses that are not acceptable to God! Thank God for men like General Booth who founded The Salvation Army and demonstrated the kindness of God to the destitute.

The heart of Jesus

Simple acts of kindness can influence people greatly, but we should not manipulate people with kindness in order to achieve certain ends. We should not have any ulterior motives; rather we should have the heart of Jesus. Kindness may mean refusing to give money to the alcoholic beggar we pass every day but perhaps we could give a sandwich or ask if we can be of help in some other way. A kind gesture or a few moments of conversation could make a tremendous difference in his day. Kindness may mean that we confront people with their problem and assist them toward finding the solution. We may not have the expertise needed but we can link people up to those who have. Kindness will always have a spiritual dimension because it would be most unkind to feed the body without feeding the soul. Kindness therefore will always be concerned about the spiritual welfare of others, but it will never neglect the physical aspect of a person's need. In the home kindness may need to be expressed in discipline rather than yielding to every whim of your child. Kindness demands wisdom and strength as well as love and compassion. May God supply the grace we need to form the habit of kindness by regular practise! In doing this by his grace we display the fruit of the Spirit!

Notes to Chapter 5

1 **Frederick William Faber** (1814–63). I am merely endorsing the words quoted and not his conversion to Roman Catholicism.

Goodness

'The fruit of the Spirit is … goodness …'

What is goodness? It may be helpful for us at this stage to put the concept of 'goodness' under the linguistic microscope. This is a beneficial exercise because it refreshes our minds on the scope of the concept. In doing this we see that goodness may be defined as virtue or excellence. It is that which is beneficial in a person or thing. Thus we speak of competence in this way when we say, 'she is good at languages' and 'he is a good at sports'. We emphasise the favourable quality of something when we say 'milk is good for you'. The word 'good' is an adjective and as such it is a word that is used to describe or modify a noun (name of person, place or thing). Thus we say 'John is a good man', 'Paris is a good city', 'Ford is a good car'. It can also be used in the same way in relation to a pronoun (a word used instead of and to indicate a noun already mentioned or known, especially to avoid repetition). For example, 'he is a good man', 'it is a good city' and 'she is a good car'. We use the word good to describe something that is effective and reliable. For example, we speak of 'good brakes'. 'Good' speaks of the quality of something, for instance, we talk about 'good food' to distinguish it from bad food or food of lesser quality. When we refer to 'good deeds' we are speaking about actions that are morally excellent and virtuous. Good refers to behaviour as an indication of character as in 'good child'. When something is enjoyable and agreeable we describe it as good, for example 'a good film' or 'good news'. The word 'good' also speaks of thoroughness; thus we say 'I gave the house a good cleaning'. When we consider our action to be valid or sound we say that we have done such and such with 'good reason'. When a person is financially sound we say 'his credit is good'. It is obvious therefore that even a brief examination of the word 'good' shows that it has a great deal of nuance and varied application in ordinary, everyday usage.

When we consider goodness as fruit of the Holy Spirit we see that it is a quality of Christian character that is about virtue and excellence. Goodness is something that is beneficial in a person. It is a word that describes a competent, effective and reliable Christian. Goodness speaks of the quality of our Christian lives. Goodness is not some internal sentiment rather it refers to the lifestyle of the Christian. Good deeds indicate goodness in our transformed characters. Our company should be enjoyable and agreeable to others. Our goodness is based on the sound condition of our blood bought souls. We have been thoroughly cleansed by Christ's blood.

Restoration of right relationship

C.S. Lewis said: 'No man knows how bad he is until he has tried to be good'. How true this is. Man in his original nature as created by God was good. Thus we read in Genesis, after man and woman had been created, 'God saw all that he had made, and it was very good.' (Genesis 1:31). As we read through the next couple of chapters we learn that man disobeyed and rebelled against God. In Eden Adam and Eve refused to be guided and governed by the Almighty and satisfied their own perverse curiosity and lust for knowledge and power. They rejected God's Word as authoritative. So man fell and in that fallen and depraved condition lost communion with God and could be no longer described as good. Through faith in Christ the believer is restored and knows that dynamic and daily communion with God. When God looks at his new creation and sees the garments of righteousness supplied through the finished work of Christ he can say again that it is 'very good'. Through Jesus there is restoration to a right relationship with God.

Goodness presents us with a problem insofar as it is a higher standard than we can achieve. In our humanity we fail but in the power of the Holy Spirit the fruit of goodness is produced. Our sanctification is not about reformation but about transformation. Our efforts to reform based on our own willpower and strength will not succeed, but the regenerative power of the Holy Spirit will begin the process that ultimately produces fruit. We cannot be imitators of Christ unless we are first conquered by the Holy Spirit and captivated by an ambition to obey the will of God as Jesus was. Changes in us, therefore, are not due to imitation or self-generated reformation but rather to the transformation, which is the result of the indwelling power of the Spirit of God. The Holy Spirit is seeking to do good things in us and through us to others.

When we talk about disposition and personality we usually mean inherited family traits. Likewise goodness is about having a good disposition that begins with having the nature of God, who is entirely good. It is about exhibiting that family trait. As such it is completely different to what we might call 'a good mood'. The vagaries of human nature are such that humours are whimsical and come and go. Moods are changeable, like the weather. The transforming power of the Holy Spirit sets about establishing a good disposition within the believer. This is an essential and indispensable part of the new personality that God is at work to produce. It is nurtured by living a life that is consistent with God's love. As such it is about loving others as God loves us. This new make-up is not just cosmetic rather it is organic and should make us easy to live with. Our new nature should make us approachable. Do we have a disposition that is marked by goodness?

Reflecting the goodness of God

Goodness is about having a good attitude. A Spirit filled person is friendly. Are we friendly and approachable? Jesus was quick to befriend the needy. He was a friend of sinners. He never condoned sin or endorsed wrongdoing but he did not reject sinners in need of his goodness. He is found in the gospels always reaching out to hurting ones, healing and helping and offering hope because he is good. That goodness characterised his ministry. The words of Peter recorded in Acts point out the connection between the operation of the Holy Spirit and doing good: 'God anointed Jesus of Nazareth with the Holy Spirit and power…he went around doing good and healing all who were under the power of the devil, because God was with him' (10:38).

Exercising goodness is about looking for the best in people and not focusing on faults. Complaining and slandering cannot coexist with goodness. We need to ask ourselves if we should have a better attitude at home, at church, at work, at college or wherever? Do we have a desire to do good for others?

Motivation

Motivation here is very important. Many people are part of religious systems where it is believed that doing good has meritorious value in terms of earning salvation and that such works will be credited to their account. They hope that the final audit will allow them access to heaven, though perhaps they dare not overtly claim to have such confidence. The reality is that they live in fear that they have not done enough to warrant a place in heaven. This completely contradicts the teaching of Scripture. In the Bible we learn that good works or observance of religious rites and rituals cannot earn salvation. Paul writing to the believers in Ephesus says, 'For it is by grace you have been saved, through faith—and this not from yourselves, it is the gift of God—not by works, so that no one can boast. For we are God's workmanship, created in Christ Jesus to do good works, which God prepared in advance for us to do' (Ephesians 2:8–10). We should note firstly that he addresses them as people who 'have been saved'. They are a people who have already been redeemed. Although there is a future eschatological dimension to that salvation, insofar as they are a people who are yet to be transported to heaven, they may have confidence in that salvation in the here and now. This is entirely consistent with the way Paul opens his letter to the church in Ephesus when he says: 'To the saints in Ephesus'. This assurance of eternal salvation is obtainable by grace alone, through faith alone, in Christ alone! Paul reminds them that salvation is something bestowed upon them by God's grace. Then he explicitly states that salvation is not achieved by works and this is such an explicit statement one wonders how any system of religious belief can deviate from such a clear statement of truth. As Jonathan Edwards put it, 'If there be ground for you to trust in your own righteousness, then all that Christ did to purchase salvation, and all that God did to prepare the way for it, is in vain.'

These verses in Ephesians comprise a truly wonderful statement. Christians should often meditate upon them because they liberate people from the treadmill of good works offered to God to earn salvation. However, Paul then goes on to explain the proper place of good works in the life of the Christian: 'For we are God's workmanship, created in Christ Jesus to do good works, which God prepared in advance for us to do' (v. 10). Salvation is never the outcome of good deeds but good deeds will invariably be the outcome of salvation. In Christ we are people who are remade. It is out of gratitude for his great grace that we become instruments of goodness in his hands. It is amazing to contemplate the idea that God has prepared good works for us to do! It is our responsibility, therefore, to seek out such opportunities to do good for others. So, although good works do not earn salvation they emerge from an internal change in the lives of those who belong to him. People who do not belong to Christ may do good works but what is their motive? If it is to earn salvation it is futile. If it is out of love for humanity (although that is very noble) it is impotent because it does not have God's glory in mind. Love for humanity without love for God is impotent. So too is faith that is not based on the revealed truth of God's word. Faith in false religion will not save. Faith itself is worthless unless it is grounded in the truth. We could say this of all the fruit of the Spirit, that there is no joy like the joy of salvation, no peace like the peace of God and so on. When James says: 'Faith without works is dead' (James 2:26, NKJV) he is challenging the integrity of those who profess faith in Christ and do not bear the fruit of goodness. He is not saying that faith and works together merit salvation. Rather he is saying that where real faith exists it will bear the fruit of good deeds.

Demonstrating goodness

Let us seize opportunities to show the goodness of God to others. We need never be at a loss to know how to do this. The world is such a needy place that there are endless ways of demonstrating the goodness of God such as, visiting the sick, caring for widows, giving to the poor, comforting those who are grieving and bearing one another's burdens. Perhaps it is time for a check-up. We need to check our disposition, attitude and our service for others. Let us ask ourselves what changes need to be made? We must then let the Holy Spirit make those changes. Josias Shute said 'a musician is commended not that he played so long, but that he played so well. And thus it is not the days of our lives, but the goodness of our lives that is acceptable unto God Almighty'. Let us play well. The more we practise the better we will play. May we be a people who are commended by God and recognised by all as those who bear the fruit of goodness! We should have that 'readiness to do good for all as we have opportunity' (Matthew Henry).

Real goodness is rooted in godliness. We remind ourselves again that Jesus is the most wonderful illustration of goodness: 'he went about doing good' (Acts 10: 38, ESV). We all fall short of Christ in this regard. As Alexander Maclaren said, 'Every man has far more knowledge of good than he uses.'

Nevertheless God has prepared good works for us to do. We must allow ourselves to be directed by him to do good. James points out the hypocrisy and contradiction inherent in a spiritual life that is merely an intellectual assent to the veracity of doctrine or an emotional engagement that is disconnected from doing good. Thus he says: 'Who is wise and understanding among you? Let him show it by his good life, by deeds done in the humility that comes from wisdom' (James 3:13). Heavenly wisdom is more than knowing truth it is also about bearing good fruit. Thus James goes on to say: 'But the wisdom that comes from heaven is first of all pure; then peace-loving, considerate, submissive, full of mercy and good fruit' (James 3:17). In Christ our consciences are quickened and in this sensitised state we perceive the needs of others in a new way. We are called to be faithful to this operation of the Spirit within us. It is an offence to God to be indifferent to the needs of others. It grieves God when we ignore opportunities to bear the fruit of goodness. So a little further on in James we read, 'Anyone, then, who knows the good he ought to do and doesn't do it, sins' (James 4:17).

Goodness is recognised and admired by others and we should do all that we can to ensure that God gets the glory he deserves through the fruit of goodness in us and through us to others. As Christians we should not only take the moral temperature of the world but we should regulate that moral temperature. We should influence the moral climate of our communities through our goodness.

The Christian is a beneficiary of God's goodness in Christ and has the reasonable expectation that God's goodness will attend him throughout his days. This is not to suggest that the Christian will live a trouble-free life. Rather that God's goodness will pursue him and looking back he will know that God's paths are best, even if painful. The Christian can say with the psalmist, 'Surely goodness and love will follow me all the days of my life' (Psalm 23:6). Although we do not know what the future may hold, yet we know the one who holds the future and his ways are good.

Chapter 6

Defining goodness

We cannot take our standard of goodness from humanity. As Christians our notion of goodness (being good and doing good) is quite different to that of the world. God is good (Psalm 100:5) but humans are not inherently good and even people who have been soundly converted to Christ face internal struggles between their old nature and their new. Thus the great apostle Paul said of himself: 'I know that nothing good lives in me, that is, in my sinful nature. For I have the desire to do what is good, but I cannot carry it out. For what I do is not the good I want to do; no, the evil I do not want to do—this I keep on doing. Now if I do what I do not want to do, it is no longer I who do it, but it is sin living in me that does it' (Romans 7:18–20). We can all relate to the reality of Paul's struggle because we know that our hearts are battlefields where good and evil are constantly at war. We know the turmoil of divided hearts. Our sinful nature is nailed to the cross but we should be aware that crucifixion is a slow death and that the old nature lingers on until we go to be with Christ. Later on in the same epistle he tells us to 'cling to what is good' (Romans 12:9). In these words too we get a sense of how difficult it is to maintain goodness. Nevertheless we must make a determined effort and this point is reinforced later in the same chapter where he says: 'overcome evil with good' (Romans 12:21).

What an enormous challenge this presents to believers in every generation but none more so than today. It is quite distressing at times to read the newspaper, watch the television news or listen to the radio news broadcasts. Christians should be involved in the caring professions, medicine, social work, rehabilitation, education and so on. We must go beyond our personal distress and allow our prayers to take us into contact with the victims and perpetrators of evil that we might do what we are commanded to do and overcome evil with good! What are we doing about domestic violence, child abuse and the litany of evil that litters our moral world? There is much evil that is abhorrent to most people but there is evil, by biblical standards, that is acceptable according to society's secular standards. We must detest all evil, even if it is deemed to be acceptable in our world.

Many people today think that they are basically good people and that because God is good he will allow them into heaven on the basis of being basically more good than bad. This is not Christian teaching even if certain denominations that adhere to this view profess to be Christian. These views are not biblical. This truth is seen in the Old Testament in Isaiah where we read, 'all our righteous acts are like filthy rags' (64:6). The book of Hebrews makes it clear that the Old Testament sacrifices and priesthood were a token of the reality of Christ's redemptive work which was enacted *once*, for *all* time. So God is good and his actions consistently reveal this and none more so than laying down his sinless life for sinners at Calvary.

Scripture has much to say about the goodness of God. His created world was good (Genesis 1:31). His laws are good (Psalm 19:7) and his goodness is worked out in our lives as we walk in his will (Romans 12:2). Psalm 107 invites us to, 'Give thanks to the LORD, for he is good' (v. 1) and then it goes on to tell us about God's goodness. At a literal level it may be read as a record that recalls God's goodness to his people in delivering them from Babylonian captivity after seventy years. However, it may also be seen as an exposition on the theme of redemption in a general, spiritual sense and as such it is a perfect meditation on this theme. God's Word frequently defines what is good by describing it in contrast to what is evil. This is so in the very passage of Scripture that we are considering where the fruit of the Spirit is contrasted with the 'acts of the sinful nature' (Galatians 5:19–23). However, God does not just define and describe goodness, he demonstrates it. The fact of Calvary in the history of humanity clearly demonstrates God's goodness, holiness, justice and love. The Bible is essentially a book about the goodness of God overcoming evil. God overcame Satan through the cross. God overcomes evil through the salvation and sanctification of individuals in every nation and generation. God's goodness is revealed in his Word, his work and his will, working in harmony for the good of humanity and his inestimable honour.

Acceptable goodness

Faithful obedience to the revealed will of God through his Word is acceptable goodness. In the book of Deuteronomy we read: 'Be careful to obey all these regulations I am giving you, so that it may always go well with you and your children after you, because you will be doing what is good and right in the eyes of the LORD your God' (12:28). God's people are called to lives of righteousness. That involves turning our backs on evil and pursuing what is good (Psalm 34:14). The children of God are to actively seek goodness and shun evil and are called to love goodness and hate evil (Amos 5:14–15). The Lord is willing to bless those who are given over to goodness as Proverbs states: 'A good man obtains favour from the LORD' (12:2). We are called to good deeds, not as a means of earning salvation but as a way of exhibiting the reality of that salvation. Jesus exhorted his disciples toward good works when he said, 'In the same way, let your light shine before men, that they may see your good deeds and praise your Father in heaven' (Matthew 5:16). Jesus preached about the necessity of bearing good fruit (Mathew 7:15–33) and doing good even in very difficult circumstances (Luke 6:27–36, a passage about loving our enemies). Evil must be crushed if good is to be cultivated. We will not suddenly become good in the face of some great opposition or oppression unless we have formed the habit of shunning evil and savouring good.

Goodness begins when we come to know God's eternal goodness in our lives. God's general goodness may easily be taken for granted and he may not be acknowledged as the source of such goodness. This general goodness is imparted to us in the rain and the nutrients of the soil that make crops grow. Every moment of life and health is from God the author of life and the one who sustains life. But more than this God's special goodness is given to us in the person of Jesus and the redemption he provides to those who believe in him for salvation. If God's general goodness was taken away this world would be a miserable place to inhabit and if we do not avail of his special goodness in Christ the next world will be very miserable indeed.

Regulating religion

So God is good and goodness is the fruit of his Spirit. How can we know what is good and acceptable to God? There is no moral consensus in the world today and even Christians may be divided on what is right and what is wrong. We live in an age very much like that of the time spoken of in Judges where it says: 'every man did that which was right in his own eyes' (17:6, AV). The only way of knowing what is good and what is evil is to allow the Word of God to guide and govern us in all matters of faith and practice. It must regulate our religion and our reasoning about issues we face in society.

The natural inclination of man's heart is toward wickedness. Thus Jeremiah writes: 'The heart is deceitful above all things' (17:9). We cannot and we dare not trust our own judgement. Our discernment must be rooted in the counsel of his infallible, inerrant, authoritative and efficacious Word. Proverbs cautions us about following the inclinations of our hearts rather than the mind of God: 'There is a way that seems right to a man, but in the end it leads to death' (14:12). We cannot be moral chameleons who adapt to whatever environment or culture we inhabit. The only situational ethics we can legitimately speak of is ethics situated in Scriptural principles! It is not easy to be good in a bad world. Our thinking may become warped in this world, and that is one reason why we need the Word of God as it helps us to keep an eternal perspective in earthly circumstances. We live in a pluralist society where the very concept of objective, absolute truth is perceived not just as antiquated but absurd. Epistemological and ethical fragmentation has led to moral relativism. All that relativism has to offer is ruin and eternal regret. In this context the only compass we have is the Word of God. Age-old Christian values that have held the fabric of society together are discarded and we might well ask with the psalmist: 'When the foundations are being destroyed, what can the righteous do?' (Psalm 11:3). We must help others to see that God is good and that his Word is good and wise and wonderful!

God is good

God is not just superlatively good because he is not just *better* than his creation or *the best* in relation to his created beings, rather he is qualitatively different in that he is altogether other. There is no flaw or failing in him. On one occasion when Jesus was addressed as, 'Good teacher' (Matthew 19:16, NKJV) he responded with these words: 'Why do you call me good? … No one is good but one, that is, God' (Matthew 19:17, NKJV). Because only God is good any goodness that we might manifest must come from him. This is what happens when we walk in the Spirit and bear fruit out of that constant communion with the Spirit. The original Greek word used in Galatians 5:22 for goodness is; *agathosune*. This is an unusual word that combines the idea of being good and doing good. That intrinsic quality of the Spirit of God will reveal itself in acts of goodness.

Goodness is rooted in the Godhead and is more than the aspiration or achievement of high ethical standards. It can only come from a good heart where the righteousness of Christ has been imputed, a heart inhabited by the Holy Spirit.

The word 'goodness' is used thirteen times in the Old Testament (nine of those occasions in the Psalms) and seven times in the New Testament, twice in one verse (2 Peter 1:5). All of the Old Testament references relate to the goodness of God. They speak of confidence in his unfailing goodness and wonder at his great goodness. Some appeal to God on the basis of his goodness whereas others express thankfulness for his goodness. In the New Testament the writer to the Hebrews also speaks of the goodness of God and acknowledges that the believer is a recipient of that goodness through the Scriptures when he says that we, 'have tasted the goodness of the word of God' (Hebrews 6:5). Paul says of the Romans that they were 'full of goodness' (Romans 15:14). Here he is commending them for the grace of God evident in their lives. He tells the Ephesians that the 'fruit of the light consists in all goodness' (Ephesians 5:9). In other words: when the light of God banishes darkness the outcome will be evidenced in the outworking of the goodness he instils within us. Peter speaks of God's 'glory and goodness' (2 Peter 1:3) and in his second epistle says: 'make every effort to add to your faith goodness' (2 Peter 1:5). In all of these references as well as our text in Galatians 5 we see the inseparable unity of God's goodness and the expression of it in Christian conduct. That conduct comes from character transformed by grace. The call to goodness is an insuperable challenge without such grace.

The problem of humanism

According to the prevailing worldview promulgated by many pagan priests of psychology,[1] people are inherently good. This kind of humanism influences education, false religion, psycho-social therapies, the criminal justice system, art, literature and every other sphere of life. Does it get into the church too? We need to understand that man is not inherently good, he is not born good and the natural inclination of his heart is toward evil. This is what the Bible teaches. Sadly in many of today's churches people in the pews are not being taught to think biblically by having their erroneous and worldly views challenged from Scripture. Nevertheless we thank God for those churches where the biblical view is upheld. The world says that people are born 'good' but the environment in which they are nurtured causes them to behave badly. There is no doubt that nurture may contribute to bad behaviour but as Christians we do not accept the view that people are, by nature, good. Everybody is born in sin and has an innate tendency for wrongdoing and a propensity for evil. Paul tells us, 'all have sinned and fall short of the glory of God' (Romans 3:23). David said, 'Surely I was sinful at birth, sinful from the time my mother conceived me' (Psalm 51:5). Because Adam sinned, all those descended from Adam inherit his rebelliousness against God. Paul teaches this truth to the Corinthians, 'in Adam all die' (1 Corinthians 15:22). The evidence speaks for itself. This world is a place where greed and exploitation is prevalent in every society. It is a place where every form of imaginable evil is endemic. The utopia promised by the paradigm of modernism has never been delivered. That is why we now live in an age of postmodern disillusionment and cynicism.

This rather bleak situation can only be remedied when we acquire a new nature in Christ. This is what it means to be born again. Thus Paul writes, 'Therefore, if anyone is in Christ, he is a new creation; the old has gone, the new has come' (2 Corinthians 5:17). We are not redeemed because God sees some merit in us or because we have some indispensable talent that might be useful in his kingdom. Neither are we saved as a result of God's foresight or foreknowledge whereby God sees that sometime in the future we will acknowledge Christ as Saviour and Lord. In the light of that knowledge he decides to redeem us. This, though a popular view, is not a Scriptural position. Rather Scripture clearly teaches the doctrine of unconditional election. A correct understanding of this truth is crucial to understanding the nature of goodness as fruit of the Spirit. It relates also to the doctrine of the total depravity of mankind. We need to understand that our salvation was God's choice and it is helpful for us to know when it was settled and on what basis it was made. Understanding our election in these terms assists our worship of God, stimulates holiness in living and informs and motivates evangelism. We must be thoroughly disabused of the notion that our salvation is about God releasing a dormant or latent goodness within us. If we are to understand goodness as fruit of the Spirit we must understand that our election is unconditional.

God's choice—when it was settled, on what basis it was made

Many Scriptures attest to the biblical truth that the salvation of souls is God's choice (e.g. John 15:16; Acts 13:48; Romans 8:29–30; Ephesians 1:4–6, 11–12; 2 Thessalonians 2:13). Furthermore, Scripture tells us when that choice was made: 'For he chose us in him before the creation of the world' (Ephesians 1:4).

So the doctrine of predestination is clearly taught in Scripture. Those who would seek to deny it are not being faithful exegetes of these texts. However, in an effort to dilute this teaching (which is, in essence, an attempt to deny it) many have sought to redefine the term *predestination*. Perhaps the most grievous misinterpretation of this glorious truth is the equation of predestination with God's foreknowledge. This is a serious distortion that is injurious to the truth of the gospel. Although it is a notion that has found widespread acceptance it is utterly odious to God. Calvin says: 'Men do not gain the favour of God by their free-will, but are chosen by his goodness alone before they were born' (Calvin's *Commentary* on Hosea 4:18, 4:19): this clearly states when God's choice was made and on what basis it was made.

Peter, in his second epistle, speaking of Paul says: 'His letters contain some things that are hard to understand, which ignorant and unstable people distort' (3:16). There is a correlation between ignorance and instability and the outcome of both is a distortion of the truth. Many people who countenance the idea of an omniscient God who foresees how people will respond to the truth of the gospel and predestines to eternal life those whom he foresees responding in faith are merely ignorant of Scriptural truth. The New Bible Dictionary says: 'The contemporary evangelical church has become largely Arminian often as a result of anti-doctrinal bias rather than careful theological reflection. The historic Augustinian doctrine of predestination remains biblically and theologically compelling' (p. 530). But there are also intellectual advocates of this view, a vanguard who intentionally and vehemently admonish others to consider the Augustinian/Calvinistic view as invalid. We respect the right of others to hold, in good conscience, a different view on this issue and acknowledge that we are brethren in Christ. We would not want to question their integrity but we do attribute such belief to poor judgement. So we can say that there are varying degrees of Arminianism ranging from the intellectually vacuous to the intellectual vanguard and somewhere in between there are those who vacillate.[2] If we appear uncharitable to those who hold Arminian views it is out of a desire to prompt serious consideration of this issue and its implications.

The key verses in the Arminian armoury are 2 Thessalonians 2:13 and Romans 8:29–30. They seem to support their position regarding foreknowledge. However, God's foreknowledge does not merely mean knowledge in advance of some event happening (prescience). God's foreknowledge is knowledge based upon a plan. As such it means not just to know beforehand but to love beforehand (fore-love).

In Romans 9:14 Paul asks the question 'Is God unjust?' The resounding answer exclaimed by the apostle is 'Not at all!' If unconditional election is not being taught in Romans 9, why raise and answer this question? Obviously Paul is anticipating objections to this teaching and addresses the issue. He is addressing a charge that presupposes he will be understood as teaching unconditional election. If Paul were teaching universal election or divine election without that unconditional element nobody would raise a question about God's fairness. The issue of the injustice of God never arises in the Arminian theory because it is seen as a judicious foreordination. Paul does not equivocate on the issue and he does not present a rational explanation to pacify doubters. He simply states 'Not at all!' Don't say it and don't think it because it is not true. Verse sixteen directly addresses the Arminian issue: 'It does not, therefore, depend on man's desire or effort, but on God's mercy'. Man is free to make choices but that freedom is limited by his fallen nature. He has only his perverse rational powers to guide him to follow his depraved inclinations.

Socinus (1539–1604), the forerunner of Unitarianism, who was deemed to be a heretic by the Christian church, translated Scripture in a manner that suited his theories. Acts 13:48 says: 'all who were appointed for eternal life believed' but he put it in the reverse order 'all who believed were appointed for eternal life'. This distortion of Scripture is popular today.

The Canons of Dort forged in Holland (1618–1619) countered what was

Chapter 6

deemed to be a Pelagian heresy. This Synod was convened to determine doctrine threatened by Arminianism and countered the view that election is based on God's foreknowledge. In repudiating this position the Canons set forth the Reformed doctrine of unconditional election.[3]

Arminianism is a man-centred theory like the pre-Copernican worldview which held that the earth was the centre of the universe. Whereas Calvinism, is a God-centred perspective that could be likened to the Copernican system where the planets, including the earth, are understood to move round the sun. Election is not merely a ratification of man's decision. As John Owen put it, 'Christ did not die for any upon condition, if they believe; but he died for all God's elect, that they should believe.' What is truly amazing in election is not that God chose some but that he chose any! We have no desire to be uncharitable to our Arminian brethren and we would all do well to remember that one day Calvinists and Arminians will ultimately inhabit Heaven together!

Since the fall of Adam man in his lost and sinful condition is at enmity with God. His fallen and rebellious nature is so corrupted that he has neither the desire nor the inclination to seek after God. Salvation, therefore, must, of necessity, come from God's gracious initiative. Calvin said: 'God ... wrote the names of his children in the Book of life before the creation of the world; but he enrols them in the catalogue of his saints, only when, having regenerated them by the spirit of adoption, he impresses his own mark upon them' (Calvin Commentary on Psalm III: 403). This view of the sequential order of election and adoption is consistently expressed by Calvin '[God's] secret election precedes adoption' (Commentary on Romans: 239).

The election of a soul to salvation does not depend on any residual virtue or moral excellence in the individual. A person is elected to salvation in accordance with God's sovereign purpose by his eternal and inscrutable decree. It is based on the goodwill and pleasure of God alone. As to when God's choice was settled we uphold Calvin's view that, 'The election of God is anterior to Adam's fall' (Calvin Commentary on Zechariah-Malachi: 477).

Election and reprobation

The reason why some are rescued while others are passed over is a mystery to the rational mind that seems to breach our understanding of the notion of justice. To some God may appear to be capricious and even callous. But there is nothing whimsical or arbitrary in God's choice. Election is not the random and despotic action of an indifferent God. Rather it magnifies his grace. Grace has often been presented as God's unmerited favour to the undeserving but that is a definition that fails to fully explain the true nature of grace because grace is, rather, God's unmerited favour, not to the *undeserving*, but to the *Hell-deserving*! The reprobate, therefore, receive what they deserve and the seriousness of sin is stressed in their eternal punishment.

The consideration of such a mysterious matter demands modesty. Spurgeon said 'I have never set up to be an explainer of all difficulties and I have no desire to do so.'[4] His exemplary humility should set the tone for any consideration of this issue. Calvin too had a sense of inadequacy when contemplating this topic. He said: 'Nor let us be ashamed to be ignorant of some things relative to a subject in which there is a kind of learned ignorance' (*Institutes* III: xxi.2).

Are we who value the truth of election as taught by Augustine and Calvin sometimes rather vain and conceited in our efforts to be valiant champions of this Doctrine of Grace? Consider Calvin's words: 'To those whom [God] devotes to condemnation, the gate of life is closed by a just and irreprehensible, but incomprehensible, judgement' (*Institutes* III: xxi.7). If a great spiritual soul like Calvin with his powerful intellectual faculties believed in election but admitted that it was 'incomprehensible' would it not be wise for us to have a similar attitude?

It is right to be unequivocal and unashamed of this glorious truth as the authentic teaching of Scripture but it is ugly when there is a haughty spirit where humility would be more appropriate. The keynote for a befitting attitude to the profundity of predestination may well be taken from Paul's great doxological statement: 'Oh, the depth of the riches of the wisdom and knowledge of God! How unsearchable his judgements, and his paths beyond tracing out! Who has known the mind of the Lord?' (Romans: 11:33–34). However, we must assert this truth in love, not only to affirm our own faith but also to establish others in a truly biblical understanding of election. This understanding is foundational for our understanding of goodness.

Spurgeon goes on to talk about how some medicine is better swallowed than chewed. He says: 'In the same way there are some things in the Word of God which are undoubtedly true which must be swallowed at once by an effort of faith, and must not be chewed by perpetual questioning.'[5] It is crucial to have a correct view of goodness if we are ever going to manifest this fruit of the Spirit.

How does this doctrine assist worship of God?

Consider the fact that God's choice was made before the foundation of the world and that it is an act of pure and absolute grace. Consider how our sins deserve his wrath and yet he bestows grace upon grace. Consider, in the words of the Canons of Dort how: 'He did this in Christ ... to justify them, to sanctify them, and finally, after powerfully preserving them in the fellowship of his Son, to glorify them.' What is the outcome of such meditation? Are we not moved to a profound sense of gratitude? Surely these thoughts stimulate love and devotion in our hearts and goodness will inevitably be the outcome!

This glorious truth also prevents us from any inclination to put ourselves in the centre of the frame and compels us to worship with a right perspective by being centred on God. Hymns written from this understanding are free from the egocentricity that characterises *some* modern choruses. How can this doctrine inspire anything other than awe in humble hearts?

Furthermore we worship God by understanding and upholding this truth in preaching and prayer. Martin Luther said: 'to know God is to worship him' and from this we understand that our worship of God is an expression of our understanding, a response to his revelation. Worship is rooted in doctrine and to be enlivened by the Spirit that same Spirit must first enlighten us.

Let us remember too that worship is not just something that takes place in the Sunday church services. God is worshipped by lives that are lived for his glory in a manner consistent with his counsel.

A proper understanding of election as it relates to goodness gives us a true sense of the magnitude of God's grace and we are irresistibly prompted to offer our service as an expression of gratitude, love and worship to God.

How does this doctrine stimulate holiness in living?

A true understanding of our election to eternal life is a profound incentive for holiness in living. J. C. Ryle said: 'Election is always to sanctification. Those whom Christ chooses out of mankind, he chooses not only that they may be saved, but that they may bear fruit that can be seen'. Those who have been redeemed from the tyrannical rule of Satan ought to volitionally submit to the tender rule of Christ. In the words of Calvin: 'The object to be gained by election is, that they who were the slaves of Satan may submit and devote themselves unreservedly to God' (Calvin, Isaiah III: 255). We are saved in order to display the glory of God. Again Calvin sums it up: 'The end of our election is that we may show forth the glory of God in every possible way' (Calvin, Isaiah III: 345). A heart that appreciates the magnitude of God's grace in election is a wellspring that sustains holy living. Calvin puts it like this: 'Our holiness flows from the fountain of divine election, and … is the end of our calling' (Calvin, Corinthians I: 53).

How does this doctrine inform and motivate evangelism?

Understanding that our election is entirely unconditional (nothing to do with our goodness) ought to inspire rather than inhibit evangelism. We have a duty to desire all men to be saved and this attitude will inform and motivate our evangelism. Calvin says: 'As we cannot distinguish between the elect and the reprobate, it is our duty to pray for all who trouble us, to desire the salvation of all men' (Calvin, Psalms IV: 283). In praying for all to be saved and preaching to all as if they might be saved we leave their election to God's eternal and inscrutable discretion. Calvin says: 'The prayers which we offer for all are still limited to the elect of God … We leave to the judgement of God those whom he knows to be reprobate' (Calvin, John II: 173).

Election and reprobation are Scriptural (Romans 9:10–23) but that should not be understood as a determinism that produces fatalism in the believer. We must bear in mind that God has appointed preaching and evangelism as the means by which he will accomplish his saving purposes. Our understanding of election should not restrict our preaching. This is a crucial matter and it seems strange that an appreciation of this truth can have the effect of gagging gospel preaching. Iain Murray addresses this issue: 'While Reformed Confessions may begin with statements on the doctrine of God and divine decrees; that is not where preachers and teachers need to begin in addressing men about salvation.'[6] He points out that in the apostolic and evangelistic preaching of Acts no mention is made of the doctrine of election but that the epistles emphasise this truth. He then says: 'In accordance with this approach, Calvin, in the later editions of his Institutes, moved his treatment of election to follow teaching on justification. He recognised that Scripture generally introduces the doctrine of election to show believers the security and certainty of their salvation.'[7]

Evangelism should be motivated primarily by a concern for the glory of God and obedience to Christ's commission (Matthew 28:19). It ought to be a spontaneous outworking of our gratitude for God's grace and goodness imputed to us. It must be inspired by a concern for the eternal destiny of souls.

Rebirth not renewal

So we are not redeemed because we are good but because God is good. Thus Scripture says: 'But God demonstrates his own love for us in this: While we were still sinners, Christ died for us' (Romans 5:8). Redemption is not an awakening of the goodness within us; it is not a renewing of our nature, however radical that might be. It is a new birth. This is what Jesus told a religious leader of his day: 'I tell you the truth, no-one can see the kingdom of God unless he is born again' (John 3:3). It is a message that needs to be unashamedly proclaimed today, not only to the 'un-churched' but also to religious people and their hierarchy. Unless we are born again we cannot have fellowship with God because we are alienated from him. This enmity with God means that we are dead in our trespasses and sins. When we are born again we are reconciled to God (2 Corinthians 5:16–21) and justified in Christ (Romans 3: 26) and we come under the influence of the Holy Spirit (Romans 8: 9). God is working out his purposes through those he has redeemed. This is what Paul told the Philippians that it is, 'God who works in you to will and to act according to his good purpose' (2:13). God has started to do something very special in the heart of every believer. He has begun a process of radical transformation. That process may be very dramatic where quantum leaps forward are evident soon after conversion or it may be gradual and barely perceptible. Whatever the pace the scope is great and one day that work will be finished. We may be sure that what God has commenced he will continue until it is complete. Thus Paul reassures the Philippian believers that they may be 'confident of this, that he who began a good work in you will carry it on to completion until the day of Christ Jesus' (Philippians 1:6). The Spirit is producing goodness out of the eternal nutrients of the divine heart. When we come to faith in Christ we are instantly redeemed from the consequences of sin because Christ has borne our punishment for us (Romans 6:18; 2 Corinthians 5:17; Ephesians 2:4–6; Colossians 3:1–3). In this sense our sanctification is instantaneous. Although we no longer face the penalty of sin we continue to live in this world where there is still the presence of sin. Old habits are not easily changed and we need to be set free from these tendencies. In this sense our sanctification is a process whereby we are being progressively transformed into the likeness of Jesus (2 Corinthians 3:18). Our growth in God's grace ultimately brings glory to the Almighty (2 Peter 3:18) as we demonstrate his goodness in a world that desperately needs it. May the goodness of God attend all our ways in all our days so that we may say with David: 'Surely goodness and love will follow me all the days of my life' (Psalm 23:6).

The place of good deeds
God desires that we do good deeds but good deeds offered to God, as meritorious works to earn salvation are profoundly insulting to God. If we are to live good lives we are to do so in accordance with the counsel of his Word. We assert that the Bible is God's handbook on Christian living and that, 'All Scripture is God-breathed and is useful for teaching, rebuking, correcting and training in righteousness, so that the man of God may be thoroughly equipped for every good work' (2 Timothy 3:16–17). Good deeds, therefore, must fit in to the place God approves. Firstly, we must acknowledge the authority of the Scriptures and recognise that they are not just the supreme authority in all matters of faith and practice but that they are the only authority! If we allow God's Word to teach us, censure us and rectify any wrong thinking that we might have then we are being trained for

righteous living. Goodness which follows from this is biblical. Our motivation in doing good must be a natural outworking of his nature in us and inspired by a desire to glorify him.

It amazes me that many so called 'Christian' books from 'evangelical' stables hold Mother Theresa up as a model of Christian practice in the area of doing good. Such admiration for 'goodness' as an expression of Roman Catholic theology is seriously misguided and I offer this chapter as a corrective to what can, at best, be described (charitably) as biblical ignorance. Any religious system that promotes doing good as a means to an end (particularly if that end is salvation) is really only developing people's ulterior motives and displeasing God. Mother Theresa was undoubtedly a kind human being who showed great compassion for the poor, rejected and sick. We may have the greatest admiration for her humanitarian spirit and we may readily acknowledge the very positive contribution she made to the physical welfare of so many destitute people in giving them help and hope when others did not. Nevertheless we must remember how God views good deeds offered as meritorious works toward salvation. In relation to this his Word says: 'all our righteous acts are like filthy rags' (Isaiah 64:6).

Good thoughts

Paul tells us to meditate on good things. In Philippians he says: 'Finally, brothers, whatever is true, whatever is noble, whatever is right, whatever is pure, whatever is lovely, whatever is admirable—if anything is excellent or praiseworthy—think about such things' (4:8). What could better occupy our thoughts than his precious Word because it is true, noble, right, pure, lovely and admirable and because it is his revealed mind to mankind! The input/output principle applies here. If we meditate on God's Word we will become wise and good and if we are fixated with what is untrue we will become foolish and evil. If we are saturated in his Word we will have some understanding of our good God and our goodness will always reflect that and glorify him.

Good choices

In our lives we have many choices to make and we all face moral dilemmas at some time or another. It is important, therefore, that we, as Christians, develop biblically informed consciences that are sensitive to the mind of the Lord. This should permeate every area of our lives so that we desire ethical economics, conscientious commerce and proper politics that puts people before profits. We must not think of goodness as merely an idealistic and unachievable ideal. It is a standard of excellence to which every Christian must aspire. It is not good enough to say that we are locked into economic systems that create, sustain and perpetuate injustices in this world and that we cannot change these structures. We cannot be complacent or indifferent about the absence of goodness and we ought not to resign ourselves to the fact that greed will win. People have purchasing power and as voters or as people who abstain from voting we are participants in political agendas. It is our moral responsibility, therefore, to do all that we can to ensure that goodness prevails. Christians must be courageous in their choices and lead a lost world in the right way. It all too easy to conform to conventions but the Christian may have to be a conscientious objector even if such dissent leads to being misunderstood and becoming a dissident voice in a dark world.

Consider Daniel, a stranger in Babylon, who made a decision about how he would live. He decided that he would not be overwhelmed by the prevailing culture. Nebuchadnezzar was trying to spiritually subjugate him and if he had not made a crucial decision to believe and obey God, he would have lost his identity as one of God's people. He would have become like everybody else. However we read: 'But Daniel resolved not to defile himself with the royal food and wine, and he asked the chief official for permission not to defile himself in this way' (Daniel 1:8). He is an example to all believers that we too must adhere to our Christian convictions and thereby distinguish ourselves from the crowd irrespective of the potential personal cost.

Pleasing God

Goodness is rooted in a desire to please God. If we have hearts that are full of the grace of God then his goodness will flow through us to others. The supernatural and transforming grace of God makes it natural for us to desire and demonstrate goodness.

We are urged in Scripture to 'Hate what is evil' and to 'cling to what is good' (Romans 12:9). The clear implication of this exhortation is that the believer, with a transformed mind that is being regularly tutored in the things of God (Romans 12:1–2), knows the difference between evil and good. We cannot allow our moral standards to be determined by the world, including nominal 'Christianity'. Pluralism, ecumenism, postmodernism, liberalism and feminism influence much of what we may call mainstream Christianity. We cannot take our keynote from such churches. The Christian is called to follow Christ and in many cases that will lead to the exit door of seriously compromised churches and to the entrance door of solid evangelical churches that are biblically based schools of discipleship. True goodness is different from the ecumenical soup kitchen that is ostensibly about feeding the homeless (albeit good) but in reality is primarily concerned with 'working together' and that is another agenda.

Confusion about what is evil and what is good is certainly not a new phenomenon. In Isaiah we read: 'Woe to those who call evil good and good evil …' (5: 20). Those who do not want their perverse thinking and behaviour to be brought under the scrutiny of God's Word despise goodness. Gay lobbyists, abortionists, radical feminists, and other groups are committed to what they see as the liberalisation of society from the antiquated mores of a bygone Christian era. But the kind of world they seek to create is not in keeping with God's universal moral laws as outlined in Scripture. There is an inherent and obvious media bias that works against the true Christian perspective. We cannot be altogether surprised or dismayed by this because in the unregenerate heart there is a predisposed antipathy to God and the people of God. We need to be courageous and realise that what is commended by God as good is often condemned by the world as evil and vice versa. Peter says, 'if you suffer for doing good and you endure it, this is commendable before God' (1 Peter 2:20). This verse teaches us that doing good may be personally costly in an evil world. Nevertheless this is a price we ought to be prepared to pay so that we might please God. God is good and if his children are like him they too will be good. Let us therefore manifest the fruit of the Spirit in goodness.

Notes on Chapter 6

1 I am not condemning psychology *per se* as it can provide valuable insight to the way the mind works. Rather I am critical of its authoritative anti-Christian pronouncements when it is itself tenuously scientific.

2 These three levels of understanding can apply to Calvinists too.

3 See article seven especially.

4 Quoted from **Iain H. Murray,** 'A Crucial Text: C.H. Spurgeon on 1 Timothy 2:3–4' in *Spurgeon V. Hyper-Calvinism: The Battle for Gospel Preaching* (Edinburgh, Banner of Truth, 1995), p. 152.

5 *Ibid.,* p. 153.

6 **Iain H. Murray,** *Spurgeon V. Hyper-Calvinism: The Battle for Gospel Preaching,* pp. 115–116.

7 *Ibid.*

Faithfulness

'The fruit of the Spirit is ... faithfulness ...'

In Matthew 25 we read the Parable of the Talents. This is a very interesting and instructive passage of Scripture that sheds light on the issue of faithfulness.

Again, it will be like a man going on a journey, who called his servants and entrusted his property to them. To one he gave five talents of money, to another two talents, and to another one talent, each according to his ability. Then he went on his journey. The man who had received the five talents went at once and put his money to work and gained five more. So also, the one with the two talents gained two more. But the man who had received the one talent went off, dug a hole in the ground and hid his master's money. After a long time the master of those servants returned and settled accounts with them. The man who had received the five talents brought the other five. 'Master,' he said, 'you entrusted me with five talents. See, I have gained five more.' His master replied, 'Well done, good and faithful servant! You have been faithful with a few things; I will put you in charge of many things. Come and share your master's happiness!' The man with the two talents also came. 'Master,' he said, 'you entrusted me with two talents; see, I have gained two more.' His master replied, 'Well done, good and faithful servant! You have been faithful with a few things; I will put you in charge of many things. Come and share your master's happiness!' (14–23).

Those who are productive are commended for their faithfulness. Faithfulness is more than being custodians of what is entrusted to us. Christians are not just guardians of the truth. Christ's servants have an obligation to see the truth invested in others and producing fruit. Further on in the parable we read of the servant who buried the talent given to him. His master condemns him for this: 'you wicked, lazy servant!' (v. 26). The servants of Christ have been entrusted with the truth of the gospel and we do not please our master if we merely commit ourselves to protecting that treasure. Promoting and proclaiming the gospel is the best means of protecting it. Certainly it is precious and certainly we must protect that token of his wealth. However, if we have a maintenance mindset rather than a mission mindset this passage calls us to recalibrate our thinking so that it is aligned to the mind of God. God is the first and foremost missionary. This parable teaches us that faithfulness is fruitful.

Faithfulness is about remaining steadfast to one's commitments whether those obligations are filial, financial, legal, moral, secular or spiritual. There is much unfaithfulness in the world today. If faithfulness is rooted in character then so too is faithlessness. In other words we behave faithfully if we are intrinsically faithful people and we behave unfaithfully or faithlessly if we are unfaithful or faithless people at the core of our being. God is faithful and faithfulness is evidence of his character at work in us. Many Scriptures attest to the glorious truth that God is faithful. 'Know therefore that the LORD your God is God; he is the faithful God, keeping his covenant of love to a thousand generations of those who love him and keep his commands' (Deuteronomy 7:9). Our faithfulness begins with faith in him. It is by taking on his nature through faith that we become faithful.

Appropriate faithfulness

Being faithful in itself is not necessarily a good thing. We know from history, experience and common sense that many people manifest faithfulness to destructive ideologies, wrong causes and false religions. They may be exemplary in their faithfulness and yet misguided in adhering to the object of their loyalty. What does it mean to be faithful? If, as we have stated, God is faithful, then it may be helpful for us to understand what that means. God is faithful to himself. He is faithful to his Word. He is faithful to his love. He is faithful to his mercy. He is faithful to his justice and judgement. He keeps his covenant promises. God promises to redeem those who trust him for salvation. He will be faithful to that promise. God promises to condemn those who reject the gospel. He will be faithful to that promise. God follows through to fulfil what he desires and intends.

We are called to be faithful to his Word. It is to be our rule in all matters of faith and practice. The Christian is one who is cautioned, counselled, corrected, consoled, commended and controlled by Scripture. Faithfulness to any notion of God and his way of salvation (by grace alone, through faith alone in Christ alone) that is not based on his Word is worse than worthless because it is dangerous. The most perilous place for the soul is the place of faithfulness to falsehood! We are called to be faithful to the truth of the gospel. We are called to be faithful to the love of God. Such faithfulness accepts the veracity of that truth and responds to that redeeming love. So faithfulness as fruit of the Spirit begins with faith in God and continues in faithful relationship with him. That is the vertical dimension of faithfulness that is worked out in our horizontal human relationships.

We can trust his Word because he is trustworthy and faithful: 'For the word of the LORD is right and true; he is faithful in all he does' (Psalm 33:4). The fact that God is faithful is taught in both the Old Testament and the New Testament. Paul writing to the Corinthians says 'God, who has called you into fellowship with his Son Jesus Christ our Lord, is faithful' (1 Corinthians1:9). The first epistle of John also draws attention to this amazing attribute of God: 'If we confess our sins, he is faithful and just and will forgive us our sins and purify us from all unrighteousness' (1 John 1:9). So faithfulness is an aspect of the character of God. It is one of his main characteristics and if we are to be transformed into his likeness we too must be a faithful people. Being faithful is being like Christ and involves faithfulness to the Word of God, faithfulness to the church of Christ and faithfulness in all our relationships and responsibilities both inside and outside the household of faith. In a world where faithfulness is becoming increasingly scarce it is very reassuring to know that God is reliable. That reliability is an essential ingredient of faithfulness. When God revealed himself to Moses he proclaimed his name and nature in these words: 'And he passed in front of Moses, proclaiming, "The LORD, the LORD, the compassionate and gracious God, slow to anger, abounding in love and faithfulness, maintaining love to thousands, and forgiving wickedness, rebellion and sin. Yet he does not leave the guilty unpunished"' (Exodus 34:6–7). God keeps his promises.

Caricaturing Christ

The world (including the nominal 'Christian' world) has caricatured Christ. If we overemphasise any attribute of God to such an extent that it exaggerates the proportion of that characteristic in relation to other features of his nature then we misrepresent him. To worship such a false concept of God is idolatrous. We have all seen caricatures of politicians and celebrities in our newspapers. They are comic and grotesque representations of real and recognisable people where certain aspects of their facial features are exaggerated to ridiculous proportions resulting in a distorted picture. The real portrait of God is seen in Scripture and it is this God that we must represent and not misrepresent. The world thinks that God is so loving and gracious that he will not punish sin and that Hell is a medieval and antiquated notion which has no place in the religion of modern society. Alarmingly, this view is also gaining acceptance in the church. The world believes that all roads lead to heaven and that good deeds will earn salvation. These beliefs have no basis in the Word of God and are completely contradicted by Scripture. They are a hideous fabrication of man's mind. So, although we delight in God's promise of blessing to the elect we must not deny his promise of cursing to the reprobate. God is faithful in love and wrath. There is a Heaven and there is a Hell. The Christ of the cross of Calvary redeems and condemns. Yet those who are truly resting in his grace delight in his faithfulness: 'Because of the LORD's great love we are not consumed, for his compassions never fail. They are new every morning; great is your faithfulness.' (Lamentations 3:22–23).

Covenant keeping

In biblical history we see how God kept his commitment to never reject his people completely. Even though they were frequently unfaithful and deserving of judgement he was unwavering and constant. Immediately after Adam and Eve were banished from the Garden of Eden, God promised the Messiah. Thus we read in Genesis: 'And I will put enmity between you and the woman, and between your offspring and hers; he will crush your head, and you will strike his heel' (3:15). Here is the gospel promise that Christ would inflict a fatal blow on Satan.

God always preserved a faithful remnant, as in the time of Elijah! Even though the prophet thought he was the only one who had remained faithful to God, the Lord reminded him: 'Yet I reserve seven thousand in Israel—all whose knees have not bowed down to Baal and all whose mouths have not kissed him' (1 Kings 19:18). In every generation there are those who are faithful because of the work of the Holy Spirit. Faithfulness to God is more than not engaging in idolatry in the same way as faithfulness to one's spouse is more than not committing adultery. It is one thing to be dutiful but quite another to be devoted. Loyalty is rooted in love.

God was faithful to the people of Israel because he loved them. A loving and wise father will always keep his promises to his children. A loving father who is not wise might make a foolish promise that he cannot keep but God is not like that. God promised the land of Canaan to Abraham and his descendants and in Joshua 14 we see the distribution of that land to his descendants, the tribes of Israel.

During a famine Jacob and his family went to Egypt, where his descendants lived for more than four hundred years until the exodus. We see in the exodus event, God's deliverance of Israel from slavery in Egypt through the leadership of Moses and Aaron. This is the salvation event of the Old Testament and it is rooted in the faithfulness of the God who loved them. Canaan is more than just land, it is the inheritance promised to the Israelites by the Lord. Its conquest demonstrated God's unswerving faithfulness to his promises. It is a delight to contemplate the idea that in the New Testament Canaan is a symbol of God's land of eternal rest (heaven). This is promised to all those who believe in the Lord and trust his finished work at Calvary. God will faithfully fulfil that promise also because he is faithful in nature and in name. Thus we read in Revelation: '... These are the words of the Amen, the faithful and true witness, the ruler of God's creation' (3:14). Again this point is reinforced later in the book: 'I saw heaven standing open and there before me was a white horse, whose rider is called Faithful and True' (Revelation 19:11).

The most outstanding example of God's faithfulness is the sending of his own Son, Jesus Christ, who fulfilled all his prophetic messianic promises and will fulfil all the eschatological details of the future.

Right throughout the Bible God's faithfulness and his steadfast love and loyalty for his people are connected. Because God is faithful his Word is trustworthy. Thus we can depend on God and trust him completely. Any measurement of weights, volumes, distances, times and so on must relate to a true standard and so it is with faithfulness. That is why we have focused on the faithfulness of God so that we may come to have a true measure of the meaning of faithfulness.

When we look at the world we see much unfaithfulness and wish it could be otherwise. But we cannot expect faithfulness from people who are not possessed by the Spirit of God. Sadly the church is not immune from unfaithfulness and we long for it to be different. But the church consists of individuals and it is, therefore, the responsibility of each Christian to understand and exercise faithfulness.

An outward sign of that inward reality

We have already noted that faithfulness begins with faith. Paul tells the Romans that 'faith comes from hearing the message, and the message is heard through the word of Christ' (Romans 10:17). This is the work of the Holy Spirit who brings the lost to faith in Christ and the believer to maturity. Perhaps you have been unfaithful to God, to your husband or wife, to your family responsibilities. The work of the Holy Spirit can restore the backslider's heart. The believer's body is the temple of the Holy Spirit and the fruit the Spirit produces reveals his presence within. It is an outward sign of that inward reality. Such is faithfulness. Faithfulness proves that the believer's life is different. That hallmark of fidelity that we call faithfulness is the practical outworking of the reality of faith. Faith produces the visible evidence of faithfulness. Faithfulness to Christ, to his Word and his work in the local church is a demonstration of faith. Thus we are called to be faithful in the use of talents, gifts and material resources.

Is it not true that we delight in the faithfulness of others? When we hear missionary reports from distant lands we are encouraged by the faithfulness of our brethren to the truth of God's Word. In this regard our hearts are in harmony with that same sentiment expressed by John in his third epistle where he said: 'It gave me great joy to have some brothers come and tell about your faithfulness to the truth' (3 John 3). Christ was faithful to the truth of the Word despite hostility, ridicule and rejection. If we are to imitate the faithfulness of Christ then we must be courageous people, especially in an age of inter-faith and ecumenical endeavour.

If the believer does not have a reputation as one who is dependable, reliable and trustworthy in secular matters then who will trust him on spiritual matters. Not only will the people around him not trust him, neither will God entrust spiritual treasures to him. We must be faithful in the little things before God will assign more major responsibilities into our care. This is what Christ taught: 'Whoever can be trusted with very little can also be trusted with much, and whoever is dishonest with very little will also be dishonest with much. So if you have not been trustworthy in handling worldly wealth: who will trust you with true riches? And if you have not been trustworthy with someone else's property, who will give you property of your own?' (Luke 16:10–12).

Being faithful is about holding steadfastly to what we profess to believe. May we be able to say those words recorded in Paul's second letter to Timothy: 'I have fought the good fight, I have finished the race, I have kept the faith' (2 Timothy 4:7). We can be faithful and fixed in our hope because we follow one who is utterly dependable. This should keep us on course in our walk with God. Let us reflect on the words of the writer to the Hebrews who exhorts us to 'hold unswervingly to the hope we profess, for he who promised is faithful' (Hebrews 10:23).

Faithfulness and failure

Hebrews 11 is the great portrait gallery of faith. As we look at the names of those who are listed (people who were justified by faith) we are conscious that even great patriarchs and heroes of faith such as Abraham, Jacob, Noah, etc. were not absolutely consistent in faithfulness to God. This we may take, not as an excuse for a tardy approach to a life of faith, but an encouragement that our security in Christ depends on Christ's perfect life and sacrifice and not ours. These people made mistakes. Abraham lied when he was afraid, Jacob was a cheat and Noah succumbed to drunkenness. Their reputations may be tarnished but their relationship with God is secure. Those who love Christ will always endeavour to be faithful to him but will not succeed in living a life of sinless perfection.

Faithfulness begins with a faith that is childlike and it continues in simple trust. In Matthew's gospel we read: 'At that time the disciples came to Jesus and asked, "Who is the greatest in the kingdom of heaven?" He called a little child and had him stand among them. And he said: "I tell you the truth, unless you change and become like little children, you will never enter the kingdom of heaven. Therefore, whoever humbles himself like this child is the greatest in the kingdom of heaven"' (Matthew 18:1–4). Some people try to make faith complicated but Jesus illustrated faith with a little child. Consider how a child trusts and believes. Our faith should be childlike. This means that our attitude should be: God said it; I believe it; that settles it! Real faith places no limits on the power and love of God. Faith is built on the conviction that God can do anything and faithfulness exudes confidence and exhibits commitment. In short, faith is evident in faithfulness. Faith caused Abel to worship God (Hebrews 11:4). Faith caused Enoch to walk with God (Hebrews 11:5). Faith caused Noah to work for God (Hebrews 11:7). Faith caused Abraham to obey God (Hebrews 11:8). Faith sustains us in times of difficulty and is displayed in our faithfulness to God. We might well ask of one that is habitually unfaithful to God if in fact there is any real faith in such a life. Faith trusts that God's sovereign will is for our good and his glory. Faith trusts the providential care of God. Faith requisitions the resources of God in every crisis. Faith is not just for heroes of the past or super-saints of the present. Faith is meant to be the normal mode of life for the believer.

Real relationship makes a radical difference

Faithfulness can only come from faith and it proves the Christian's life is radically different. James emphasises this truth: 'But someone will say, "You have faith; I have deeds." Show me your faith without deeds, and I will show you my faith by what I do' (James 2:18). Faith is fidelity to the truth, fidelity to Christ, fidelity to godliness. The ultimate goal of the gospel is to bring glory to God through the godliness of the redeemed. In understanding this we also comprehend that faithfulness is the side of faith that is discerned by human perception. In other words, people do not see faith itself, but faithfulness may be visible. So faith produces visible evidence in faithfulness. Those who are faithful to Christ, his Word and his work in the local church, the use of talents and gifts and the use of material resources, bring glory to God and in so doing are fulfilling God's eternal purpose on earth and in heaven.

Faithfulness is the basis for a meaningful and enduring relationship. In the original Greek one of the meanings for this word (*pistis*) is 'trusted'. Trust is vital in any healthy relationship. To have a relationship with someone who is completely dependable and totally reliable is a very precious thing indeed. God is such a person. He is entirely trustworthy which means that he is absolutely worthy of our trust! If we want to understand the notion of faithfulness we must look to God because he is the example par-excellence of this virtue. The apostle Paul explained to Timothy that even 'if we are faithless, he will remain faithful, for he cannot disown himself' (2 Timothy 2:13). This is a wonderful verse of Scripture that reveals to us something of the very nature of God's character. God is inherently and unwaveringly faithful. The quality of his faithfulness is not contingent on the quality of our faithfulness. He is faithful to the Word of his promises. He is faithful to his holiness. He is faithful to his justice and mercy. If we are to produce this vital fruit it will only happen as a result of daily and dynamic communion with Christ, the vine.

Personal responsibility

We live in a world that is becoming more and more self-centred. It is a world where promises are frequently broken and contractual arrangements are expedient and expendable. Marriages are merely temporary arrangements with opt out clauses. Christians should be different. Each believer must take personal responsibility for faithfulness. The followers of Christ should be found to be faithful in all their relationships, with spouses, children, parents, employers, employees, friends and acquaintances. This is the lateral and social dimension of faithful obedience to God. We cannot say that we are faithful to God if we are unfaithful in our human relationships.

The world may evaluate us on our achievements and successes (educational, financial and so on) but God will appraise us on the basis of our faithfulness to what was entrusted to us. We need to think less about how people form opinions of us and we need to think more about God's estimate of our faithfulness. We should want to hear those words from his lips: 'Well done, good and faithful servant!' (Matthew 25:23). In the parable of the talents (Matthew 25:14–30) Jesus was teaching the essential truth that faithfulness will be rewarded and unfaithfulness will be punished. There is no side-stepping this issue. If we are faithful in little responsibilities we will be entrusted with the greater treasures of heaven. This is the way God operates with his people. A popular misunderstanding is that God engages the services of those who have talent and gives them great work in the kingdom. This is not true. God gives gifts (little or large) to those who will use them faithfully. Certainly a person's aptitude, interest and ability cannot be discounted, but to think that God sees a good communicator and says: 'a man as eloquent as that would make a fine preacher' is incorrect thinking. On the contrary God gives the gift and expects the preacher to be faithful in discharging the duties of that responsibility without fear or favour. Sadly there are preachers who are too diplomatic. These people are person-pleasers rather than God-pleasers. They are more concerned about church politics and inter-church politics than in boldly taking a stand. This is unfaithfulness. Church harmony and inter-church harmony, though highly desirable, is not to be preserved at any cost. The pulpit is not a place for those who are either lovers of conflict or cowards. We shall deal with this matter further under the sub-heading, 'ministerial faithfulness'.

God's faithfulness is our hope

Even in difficult circumstances we may still cherish hope in our hearts because God is faithful. Jeremiah expressed this well:

I remember my affliction and my wandering, the bitterness and the gall. I well remember them, and my soul is downcast within me. Yet this I call to mind and therefore I have hope: Because of the LORD's great love we are not consumed, for his compassions never fail. They are new every morning; great is your faithfulness. I say to myself, 'The LORD is my portion; therefore I will wait for him.' (Lamentations 3:19–24).

In the Old Testament we read of Jehoshaphat the king of Judah who, although he commenced his reign well by conscientiously obeying God (2 Chronicles 17:3–9), later formed a military alliance with Ahab, king of Israel in opposition to the will of the Lord. The outcome was disastrous and God was displeased. Nevertheless as his kingdom came under the threat of invasion he appealed to God for help (2 Chronicles 20:1–30). That appeal was based upon an understanding of God's power (v. 6) and an appreciation of his past faithfulness (v. 7). It is a prayer built upon a proper understanding of God's covenant with Abraham (v. 7) and his just character (v. 12). God's answer to Jehosaphat's earnest petition is recorded in 1 Chronicles. There we read these magnificent words:

> Do not be afraid or discouraged because of this vast army. For the battle is not yours, but God's. Tomorrow march down against them … You will not have to fight this battle. Take up your positions; stand firm and see the deliverance the LORD will give you, O Judah and Jerusalem. Do not be afraid; do not be discouraged. Go out to face them tomorrow, and the LORD will be with you (20:15–17).

The result was that the invading armies were destroyed without any military engagement on the part of Jehosaphat and his army. The Lord promised victory and the Lord delivered victory. The ultimate outcome was that the people of God 'assembled in the Valley of Beracah, where they praised the LORD' (v. 26).

Surely this is the place we come to as we behold the faithfulness of God, a place of praise! We can praise God for his past faithfulness, acknowledge his faithfulness in our present circumstances and ask him to help us grow in faithfulness to him and to others. In doing this we will begin to see the fruit of faithfulness grow in our lives. Faith is the root of our relationship with God and faithfulness is the fruit it produces through the power of the Holy Spirit. Faithfulness is evidence of mature faith.

Measuring spiritual 'success'

In the spiritual realm it is difficult to quantify or measure success. According to the world's standards many people who have laboured faithfully without seeing much or even any positive results are deemed to be failures. The church must take great care to counter such business criteria being applied in evaluating Christian endeavour. Faithfulness is what counts in God's estimation. Faithfulness will be blessed. Thus we read in Matthew: 'It will be good for that servant whose master finds him doing so when he returns' (24:46). We are called upon to engage in the work of the

Lord by being faithful to the great commission to '... go and make disciples of all nations, baptizing them in the name of the Father and of the Son and of the Holy Spirit, and teaching them to obey everything I have commanded you. And surely I am with you always, to the very end of the age' (Matthew 28:19–20).

Ministerial faithfulness

In 1 Kings 22 we read the fascinating story of Micaiah who prophesied against Ahab. It is worthwhile considering this Old Testament story because it holds before us a picture of ministerial faithfulness that is much needed today. Let us recall the detail of that story remembering that 'All Scripture is God-breathed and is useful for teaching, rebuking, correcting and training in righteousness, so that the man of God may be thoroughly equipped for every good work' (2 Timothy 3:16). The narrative begins by telling us that there had been peace for three years between Israel and Aram and that during the third year Jehoshaphat, king of Judah, went to visit Ahab, king of Israel. Ahab had been brooding on something that had taken place in the past and he spoke about this to his officers and said: 'Don't you know that Ramoth Gilead belongs to us and yet we are doing nothing to retake it from the king of Aram?' (v. 3). Ahab asked Jehoshaphat to join forces with him in attacking Ramoth Gilead against the armies of Aram. Jehoshaphat assured Ahab of his loyalty but hesitated to proceed with the proposed plan without prior consultation with the Lord. In this he showed that he desired the assurance of the Lord's favour. So in verse 6 we read of Ahab's response: 'So the king of Israel brought together the prophets—about four hundred men—and asked them, "Shall I go to war against Ramoth Gilead, or shall I refrain?" "Go", they answered, "for the Lord will give it into the king's hand."' These false prophets were employed to say things that would please Ahab because Ahab's assessment of the worth of a prophet depended on whether or not that prophet said things that were favourable to him. Thus they were unreliable because they merely said what they understood to be what Ahab wanted to hear. Jehoshaphat recognising this said: 'Is there not a prophet of the LORD here whom we can inquire of?' (v. 7). Ahab answered: 'There is still one man through whom we can inquire of the LORD, but I hate him because he never prophesies anything good about me, but always bad. He is Micaiah son of Imlah' (v. 8). Imagine the scene with the kings of Israel (Ahab) and Judah (Jehoshaphat) arrayed in their royal robes, sitting on their thrones with four hundred false prophets giving false counsel and advising Ahab to 'Attack Ramoth Gilead and be victorious' (v. 12). The person sent to summon Micaiah (the prophet of the Lord) said to Micaiah 'Look, as one man the other prophets are predicting success for the king. Let your word agree with theirs, and speak favourably' (v. 13). This advice shows that this person held the view that all prophets were self-serving. But Micaiah replied, 'As surely as the LORD lives, I can tell him only what the LORD tells me' (v. 14). So Micaiah is consulted and initially he sarcastically mimics the four hundred false prophets by agreeing with them and advising Ahab to enter battle and emerge victorious. Ahab recognises the obvious insincerity of Micaiah's words and demands the truth in the name of the Lord. Let us pick up the story from verse 20.

And the LORD said, 'Who will entice Ahab into attacking Ramoth Gilead and going to his death there?' One suggested this, and another that. Finally, a spirit came forward, stood before the LORD and said, 'I will entice him.' 'By what means?' the LORD asked. 'I will go out and be a lying spirit in the mouths of all his prophets,' he said. 'You will succeed in enticing him,' said the LORD. 'Go and do it.' So now the LORD has put a lying spirit in the mouths of all these prophets of yours. The LORD has decreed disaster for you (20–23).

Ahab ordered that Micaiah be put in prison and fed on bread and water until he returned from battle but Micaiah spoke again and said: 'If you ever return safely, the LORD has not spoken through me.' (v. 28). We are told that in the course of the battle, 'someone drew his bow at random and hit the king of Israel between the sections of his armour' (v. 34). Here is an apparently random shot directed by God to a precise spot to fulfil God's prophetic Word. Ahab bled to death in his chariot and his army scattered. He was buried in Samaria and the blood -stained chariot was washed in 'a pool in Samaria (where the prostitutes bathed), and the dogs licked up his blood, as the word of the LORD had declared' (v. 38). Jehoshaphat was later to be condemned by the prophet Jehu (2 Chronicles 19:2) for violating the Lord's will by joining forces with Ahab.

What has all this got to do with faithfulness? Clearly Micaiah was a man of God appointed as a spokesperson for the Lord. He was faithful to the Word of God in a very difficult situation. Ahab was a wicked king who despised Micaiah. From where we stand at some distance from the situation it is easy to theorise about being faithful to the Word of God. He was willing to suffer the contempt of those in authority. He was faithful to the point of willingness to suffer the serious consequences of being a dissenting voice. His attitude to his office is a challenge to all who are appointed to minister the Word of God. He proclaimed: 'As surely as the LORD lives, I can tell him only what the LORD tells me' (v. 14). Micaiah was in a pressure situation where it would have been easier to tell Ahab what he wanted to hear. Nevertheless he stood his ground and demonstrated a courageous faithfulness to his ministry as a mouthpiece of God. He respected the authority of the Almighty more than the authority of the king. His faithfulness cost him something. Faithfulness to God's Word in a faithless and fickle generation will cost those who take a stand for its authority to rule belief and behaviour. Micaiah stood against falsehood even when all around him were boldly proclaiming a different message.

Our generation desperately need men like this. The Lord will use a man who is faithful to him. It is a story that is (in parts) reminiscent of Elijah's courageous stand against the prophets of Baal on Mount Carmel. There too we see the enemies of God vanquished and the Lord's servant vindicated. We should pray that faithful people would uphold the Word of God in our crooked and perverse generation. There are many pressures to conform and the faithful minister of the Word is often accused of being narrow minded and belligerent. Those who are faithful to the teaching of Scripture may sound strident in a world that tolerates virtually everything except the claims of Christians that the unique and universal truth of God is found in his Word and in the person of Jesus. May God raise up a generation of faithful preachers.

Unfaithfulness condemned

Isaiah and Jeremiah condemn God's people for not being faithful to God. A Christian is to be a person who has a firm conviction of the truth of God's Word. This is to be acknowledged in how he lives. A Christian surrenders to the truth and allows it to influence his conduct. This is what faithfulness to the Word of God means. When we avoid allowing that Word to manage our minds we are being unfaithful through a disobedience of omission (failing to do what we know to be right) or commission (doing what we know to be wrong). Faithfulness to Scripture involves more than merely believing it to be true. We have to go beyond acknowledging its veracity by allowing it to mould us into faithful adherents of its commands.

Gentleness

'The fruit of the Spirit is … gentleness …'

The world is becoming increasingly violent. Terrorism inspired by religion and political ideology is part of modern life. The streets of our cities are not safe, especially at night where drunken brawls frequently lead to people being injured or killed. People long for peace and security but policing cannot deliver secure communities. Consider Israel and Northern Ireland as examples of highly policed places and we see that no matter how efficient policing may be it can never be completely effective.

Why are people so angry? Why is there so much aggression ranging from domestic violence to civil and international wars? There is a malady of the heart, a sickness of the soul that needs to be treated at root cause. Society's security measures are necessary but relatively ineffective deterrents that address the symptoms rather than the source of the problem.

Rebuking the rabble

Let us consider for a moment the society in which Christ lived. Palestine was occupied by a foreign power and it was a society where religious law and Roman jurisprudence often meted out the most severe punishment for sin and crime respectively. People could be flogged, stoned or crucified. One of the disciples of Christ committed an act of violence in the very presence of Jesus. On the night he was betrayed a posse of people armed with swords and clubs came to capture Christ. All the gospels record the incident but only John reveals the identity of the disciple as Simon Peter. He was armed with a sword and did not hesitate to use it by cutting off the right ear of Malchus, a servant of the high priest. Jesus instructed Simon Peter to put away his sword, rebuked the rabble by pointing out that he was not leading a rebellion and healed Malchus. Obviously Christ behaved peacefully because he was gentle in nature. The compassionate character of the Christ we encounter in the gospels reveals a meek and gentle spirit. When Jesus preached, 'Blessed are the peacemakers, for they will be called sons of God'

(Matthew 5:9) in 'The Sermon on the Mount' he preached it from a sincere and gentle heart.

It is perplexing to think that some of the areas in this world most densely populated by Christians are the most violent societies. How can it be, for example, that some cities in such places are so dangerous? In communities with many large churches one would expect some positive impact in the cause of peace by people who promote gentleness. It would not be fair to lay the blame for community violence at the door of the churches but the watching world may well see it as an appalling indictment of a people who profess to be disciples of such a gentle Saviour. I believe we need to take the call to gentleness much more seriously. We should have an evident and determined desire for gentleness. Gentleness may well mean taking a stand against aggressive approaches to solving political problems. Those who favour military action are filling the vacuum caused by the failure of diplomacy in international relations. This is resulting in the world becoming increasingly unstable. It is our duty to use whatever influence we may have to ensure that we have gentle leaders. In exercising our franchise we must measure the manifestos of those who desire political office against the biblical manifesto for peace and gentleness.

The right to bear arms
Jesus could have legitimately carried arms for his own protection in a violent society that permitted him to do so. There is no record, however, that he did. Besides, it would be ridiculous to suggest that he may have carried arms because that would be completely uncharacteristic of all that we know of Jesus. The apostle Paul in his second letter to the Corinthians appeals to this wayward church on the basis of Christ's character: 'By the meekness and gentleness of Christ, I appeal to you' (2 Corinthians 10:1). We might well appeal to some of our fellow Christians on the same basis.

It may seem to be a rather obvious point to say that one cannot manifest gentleness while at the same time carrying a lethal weapon but it appears necessary to say so! We are all prone to culture blindness when it comes to our own culture. However, it seems incredible to Christians outside the U.S.A. that the American Constitution's guarantee to its citizens that they shall have the right to bear arms, takes precedence, amongst many

Christians, over Christ's call for gentleness. 'Take my yoke upon you and learn from me, for I am gentle and humble in heart, and you will find rest for your souls' (Matthew 11:29). This view should not be misconstrued as anti-American. The numbers of firearms related deaths in the U.S.A. is *significantly* (in fact *staggeringly*) higher in percentage terms *(per capita)* than in other developed countries and indeed than in many 'underdeveloped' and 'undeveloped' countries! The world needs to see gentleness from those who profess to be disciples of Jesus. People have secular 'rights' which are spiritual wrongs. In most developed countries women have the legal right to abortion but it is wrong to exercise that 'right'. Similarly people have the legal right to engage in homosexual activity but again we say it is not right to do so. We suggest that this is how the 'right to bear arms' should be seen. Christians may have the right to bear arms but they have a duty to refrain from indulging it!

A last resort

The Christian church has a responsibility and opportunity to offer a radically different alternative to the current trigger-happy approach to solving conflict in our world. We are not promoting absolute pacifism as the ideal Christian position because there is no Scriptural warrant for such a stance. Sadly there have been times in history (and there will likely be such times again) when war becomes necessary. There are evil despots who brutalise and terrorise their own people and abuse their power by invading neighbouring countries. There are regimes that harbour hatred against other countries and seek to accumulate weapons of mass destruction with the intention to annihilate others. There are powers that would engage in 'ethnic cleansing' policies of genocide. Nevertheless war must always be the last and least favoured option. War should never be declared unless and until every other avenue has been thoroughly explored and exhausted. War should be defensive rather than offensive. Even then those who declare a 'just war' should do so with the purest motives, the greatest reluctance and the heaviest of hearts. Because the human cost (military and civilian) in terms of the suffering that will inevitably result from war is so truly awful the ultimate objective of war must, ironically, be sustainable peace itself. War must always be the last resort, in a cause that is just, where the intention is noble and likely to succeed in its goals. The means must be proportionate and non-combatants should be guaranteed immunity. The rules of the Geneva Convention on Human Rights governing the rules of engagement in times of war must be upheld and no nation on earth should be exempt from accountability for war crimes. Admittedly the post Cold-War world where Islamic fundamentalism issues *fatwa* and declares *jihad* needs to be factored into an appropriate Christian response.

Christians ought to be a people who are essentially committed to non-violence. We are to offer the other cheek to those who would strike us so that peace may prevail. Jesus calls the Christian not only to non-violence but also to proactive peacemaking. Christ demands that his disciples love their enemies and do good to those who hate them. Furthermore we are to pray for those who persecute us. Jesus practised what he preached. He was gentle to the point of not resisting betrayal, arrest, trial, sentence, flogging, mocking and execution. He did not retaliate: 'He was led like a lamb to the slaughter' (Isaiah 53:7). In his agony Christ prayed for those who nailed him to the cross, 'Father, forgive them' (Luke 23:34). This is the way of the cross and Christ invites us to follow him by taking up our cross daily. The teaching and example of Jesus calls upon the Christian to be gentle in all his relationships.

Temples of the Holy Spirit

As we consider gentleness as fruit of the Spirit it is helpful for us to remember the relationship between the Holy Spirit and the believer. It is the Holy Spirit who brings about that conviction of sin whereby we become aware of our need of the saving grace of God. On conversion the Holy Spirit enters the believer and we ought to bear this in mind. Paul asks the question of believers: 'Do you not know that your body is a temple of the Holy Spirit, who is in you, whom you have received from God?' (1 Corinthians 6:19). He goes on to point out (in the same verse) the implication of being possessed by the Spirit of God when he says: 'You are not your own'. This is entirely consistent with his teaching later on in chapter twelve when he says that the Holy Spirit baptises the believer into the body of Christ: 'For we were all baptised by one Spirit into one body' (1 Corinthians 12:13). Furthermore the Holy Spirit seals the believer until that day when his redemption is ultimately consummated. Thus Paul writes to the Ephesians: 'And do not grieve the Holy Spirit of God, with whom you were sealed for the day of redemption' (4:30). If therefore we are a people who are possessed by the Spirit of God we will be preoccupied with his glory. Gentleness brings glory to God whereas aggression brings the gospel into disrepute. Gentleness is consistent with the character of Christ whose noble name we bear and represent as Christians. Gentleness is essential to Christ-likeness and it should be the normal Christian experience.

Meekness

In the *Introduction* we indicated that *gentleness* falls short of the fullest meaning given in the original language to this dimension of the fruit of the Spirit. Here the Authorised Version's rendition *'meekness'* is preferable. Meekness certainly involves having a patient, gentle disposition but it is more than that. Christ speaks of his own disposition as meek (Matthew 11:29) and commends the meek as blessed (Matthew 5:5). It is spoken of Jesus prophetically as the Messiah King in Zechariah 9:9 and Matthew 21 draws our attention to the fulfilment of that prophecy. Meekness is a quality of great value in God's estimation (1 Peter 3:4). The Scriptural use of the word meekness has a more profound meaning than its usage in other first century Greek writing. Meekness is not merely an external mode of behaviour. Neither is meekness merely about how people conduct themselves in their human relationships. The biblical meaning of meekness goes beyond natural disposition. It is an inward grace that is exercised initially and primarily toward God. It is an attitude of heart that accepts the efficacious nature of God's dealings with us without resentment or complaint. It is associated with the word *tapeinophrosuné* (humility) and frequently follows it in Scripture (for example, Ephesians 4:2; Colossians 3:12; Zephaniah 3:12). The meek person is a humble person and does not strive and contend with God but is submissive and accepting of the divine will. Thus the meek person is confidently resigned to the will of God in all circumstances, whether they appear favourable or not. His attitude is that, 'in all things God works for the good of those who love him, who have been called according to his purpose' (Romans 8:28). Even in suffering he knows that God allows it for the chastening and purification of those whom he loves. Thus even in difficult human relationships the godly person will remain meek.

Attitude and actions

Meekness describes a condition of mind and heart whereas gentleness is more about how one conducts oneself in relation to others. In short, meekness is about attitude whereas gentleness is about actions. In this regard neither of the English words 'gentleness' nor 'meekness' actually convey the truest meaning of the Greek word *prautés*. The meekness manifested and commended by Jesus is the fruit of the Holy Spirit, which is the power of God at work in the life of the believer. The world thinks that such people are weak, pushovers who are easily exploited and manipulated. This kind of understanding of meekness is completely wrong. It is wrong because it assumes that the meek disciple of Christ lacks assertiveness. It is seen as a frailty of the feeble minded. But Jesus was meek and yet he taught fearlessly, with authority. He had power beyond measure with infinite resources at his command. He is the ultimate model of meekness and in imitating him we can accept resentment, ridicule and rejection without recrimination. Christ was selflessly consumed with the will of the heavenly Father and in that frame of mind meekness was the inexorable outcome. If we are obsessed with our own interests, personal ambitions and reputations then every personal injury and insult will elicit a response of self-justification. This kind of self-defence is conceived in a heart that is anything but meek. It is worth noting that Moses is described as 'very meek, above all the men which were upon the face of the earth' (Numbers 12:3 AV), but he was a powerful leader of great faith and courage who represented God before Pharaoh. Christ, however, is the example par-excellence of meekness. Our supreme Saviour showed meekness to a superlative degree when he endured the inquisition of an unjust trial.

A spirit of meekness

Paul appealed to the Corinthians: 'By the meekness and gentleness of Christ' (2 Corinthians 10:1). The believer is exhorted to: 'show meekness unto all men' (Titus 3:2, AV). Meekness is an appropriate adornment for the believer and we are exhorted to clothe ourselves in it (Colossians 3:12). Meekness is the right attitude for our service to God and others, even/especially with those who are ignorant and erring. Instruction and correction is to be conducted in a spirit of meekness (2 Timothy 2:25). Meekness cultivates the heart and thus our receptivity to the Word of God is enhanced with a spirit of meekness (James 1:21). Meekness is the mode of communication commended to the believer when responding to the inquiring or arguing non-Christian (1 Peter 3:15). We do well to remember that 'A gentle answer turns away wrath, but a harsh word stirs up anger' (Proverbs 15:1).

Meek learners

If we 'receive with meekness the engrafted word' (James 1:21, AV) then we become meek learners. In meekness there is an absence of pride. It is the opposite of rebellion. This is the appropriate manner in which to approach the Word of God in our daily devotions. This calls for reading the bible regularly and prayerfully. It also calls for hearing and heeding preaching consistently. It demands listening with the heart. We are to be like little children learning new things, excited, eager and expectant. We might well ask ourselves to what extent are we eager to do the will of God? Are we content to do the will of God only if it does not cost us too much? We are expected to concentrate on what God says to us and to become completely committed to his will. Meekness as fruit of the Spirit is, therefore, about welcoming biblical truth and becoming meek learners.

Meek leaders

The church of Christ today needs meek leaders. I fear that the way of the world determines our understanding of what constitutes a good leader. What value do we place on meekness when establishing criteria for leadership? It seems that many Christians are confused about what characteristics a good leader ought to have. We tend to say he must be a good orator, articulate, eloquent and fluent with a flair for communication, a person with charisma who manifests the power to inspire and attract others. Where does meekness fit in with this kind of expectation? The world looks for credentials and qualifications, creativity, initiative and enthusiasm. The world exalts proficiency, strong planning and excellent decision-making skills together with other attributes. Is this what we think of when we contemplate the qualities of leadership?

The diploma disease

We are all familiar with the economic concept of inflation where the prices of commodities increase. In recent decades there has also been a distinct trend toward educational inflation. In other words the qualifications required by occupational institutions from potential employees are continuously being redefined in an upward direction. Is there a tendency for this inclination to influence the church?

It ought to be a matter of concern that some advertised preaching/pastoral vacancies stipulate the need for a Master's Degree as a prerequisite condition for applicants. This is an unhealthy development in the body of Christ, which may be symptomatic of the diploma disease that has affected the minds of many people today. It leads to confusion where credentials are mistaken for credibility and competence for character. Ultimately this form of recruitment leads into a qualification's quagmire that is hazardous to the health of the church.

Education is a wonderful thing and many men whom God has deigned to use in the history of the church have been well educated. John Wesley and George Whitefield, for example, were graduates of Oxford University. But it is equally true that many men that were, by God's grace, instrumental in the work of the kingdom have been uneducated. D.L. Moody had very little education and Spurgeon never had any theological training. Campbell Morgan never had any ministerial training and was turned down by the Methodist ministry when he gave his trial sermon.

Applicants must be gentle and meek

What lies behind this insistence on postgraduate level education in theology? Could it be an unhealthy reliance on human ability in the cognitive domain? We need to beware of the belief that if we have a better education[1] we will be more effective Christians! On the other hand it should be noted that many churches have been harmed by insufficient attention to ministerial training and there is, undoubtedly, a necessity for formal preparation. Scripture emphasises the necessity for diligence in the study of the Word. Thus Paul counsels Timothy 'Study to shew thyself approved unto God, a workman that needeth not to be ashamed, rightly dividing the word of truth' (2 Timothy 2:15 AV). This should be the rule. An understanding of systematic theology and a historical perspective on developments and movements within the church (including error and heresy) will be immensely helpful to the man in the pulpit. It is important, however, that traditions of high standards for ministerial training should continue to make exceptions. It is certainly not desirable that the exception should become the rule but we should bear in mind that the Holy Spirit does not restrict his divine activity to men of learning. God will delight in entrusting the treasures of heaven to people who are gentle and meek.

Being with Jesus
When the Jews heard the apostles preaching they were astonished and the account of their observation is interesting: 'Now when they saw the boldness of Peter and John, and perceived that they were uneducated and untrained men, they marvelled. And they realised that they had been with Jesus' (Acts 4:13, NKJV). Yet they were conduits for the power of the Holy Spirit. People need to hear the preaching of men who have been with Jesus. A gentle and humble heart is a chamber where God delights to dwell. When Moses descended from Mount Sinai it was evident that he had been in the presence of God and 'his face was radiant because he had spoken with the LORD' (Exodus 34:29). The church needs humble-hearted, meek and gentle preachers who have had unhurried communion with God, men who radiate something of the glory of God. A man may be a candidate for the power of the Holy Spirit no matter what his level of educational attainment, especially if he is gentle and meek! Paul reminds us that we should have a spiritual perspective when evaluating a person's merits and demerits: 'So from now on we regard no-one from a worldly point of view' (2 Corinthians 5:16). Knowledge of the Saviour is more important than knowledge of the subject. Many men of learning are arrogant and proud but isn't it wonderful to meet a scholar who is meek, humble and gentle in his instruction of others?

Looking for the right qualities

In 1 Samuel 16 we read the account of the choosing and anointing of David, who in appearance was the least likely candidate. In the estimation of his own family and even in the sight of the Lord's servant, Samuel, David was not evidently qualified. As the sons of Jesse were paraded before Samuel we find the Lord's servant convinced, first that Eliab is the one on whom God's favour rests. Thus we read that Samuel said of Eliab: 'Surely the LORD's anointed stands here before the LORD' (v. 6). But the Lord counsels his servant and in the process gives Samuel a profoundly significant insight into the heart of God. So we read in verse 7: 'But the LORD said to Samuel, "Do not consider his appearance or his height, for I have rejected him. The LORD does not look at the things man looks at. Man looks at the outward appearance, but the LORD looks at the heart."' One by one Jesse's sons were presented: Abinadab followed Eliab then Shammah until we read in verse 10: 'Jesse made seven of his sons pass before Samuel, but Samuel said to him, "The LORD has not chosen these." It seems that Jesse never even considered David for such a role. Samuel had to ask Jesse, 'Are these all the sons you have?' (v. 11). David was out in the fields tending sheep and Samuel instructed that he be summoned. He arrived and we read the outcome in verse 12 where the Lord said: 'Rise and anoint him; he is the one.' It is instructive to note that after Samuel anointed David we are told: 'from that day on the Spirit of the LORD came upon David in power' (v. 13). There was nothing in David that qualified him to receive God's gracious favour. Although it is noted that: 'He was ruddy, with a fine appearance and handsome features' (v. 12) we have already been instructed that God does not consider such things as worthy attributes for service or favour. God is concerned about the condition of our hearts. Are we meek and gentle?

The deciding factor

It is one thing to take into account the qualifications of a man applying for ministry but it is quite another thing to allow those educational qualifications to be the deciding factor in determining whether or not a man may apply in the first place. I fear that the present trend in setting educational prerequisites for preachers and pastors is focusing on the external appearance and it seems to be a secular rather than a sacred approach. We need to put gentleness/meekness on the list of essential criteria for ministerial office.

It is noteworthy that Christ had nothing in his physical appearance that was particularly attractive to others. Isaiah tells us: 'He had no beauty or majesty to attract us to him, nothing in his appearance that we should desire him' (53:2). Isaiah also tells us prophetically that Jesus was 'despised and rejected by men' (53:3). We know that Christ was despised and rejected because he preached the truth and claimed to be the truth. The unique and universal claims of the gospel are anathema to those who prefer darkness to light. Perhaps Jesus was also despised because he was a carpenter! In Mark's gospel we read of the kind of response his teaching elicited from some of those who heard him preach. Thus we read: '"Where did this man get these things?" they asked. "What's this wisdom that has been given him, that he even does miracles! Isn't this the carpenter? Isn't this Mary's son and the brother of James, Joseph, Judas and Simon? Aren't his sisters here with us?"' (Mark 6:3). And they took offence at him.' Their attitude reflects contempt for the authority assumed by an uneducated carpenter!

Learning in the school of Christ

Jesus called ordinary men to play significant roles in disseminating the message of the gospel. Men like Simon, Andrew, James and John were called to leave their fishing nets and boats behind and follow Christ. They were simple, untrained men. One might argue that they spent three years learning from the Master before they were commissioned but that was more like an informal mentoring arrangement than a structured educational programme of study with a recognised and accredited qualification at the end! There were men of learning at the time of Christ. The Scribes and Pharisees were such a class but they were far from being meek and gentle. The apostle Paul was an eminent Pharisee with a notable pedigree (Philippians 3:4–6) but God broke him in order to bless him and he became meek and counted his achievements and pedigree as nothing. He had been a student of the great Gamaliel (Acts 22:3) and he was commissioned to the work of the gospel by God (Acts 9:15). Paul was not the only educated member of the first century church, Luke, for instance, was a physician.

Consider 1 Corinthians 1:18–2:5. This passage helps us to have a biblical perspective on the issue. It is important to note that the text says: 'Not *many* of you were wise by human standards' (1:26, emphasis added) it does not say 'Not *any* of you were wise by human standards.' An educated man should not be debarred any more than an uneducated man should be considered ineligible. Even by human standards it is unwise to think that educated people have a monopoly on competence and it is naive to confuse education with wisdom.

A need for today

Perhaps one might suggest that times have changed and the general level of education in the average congregation is higher than ever it was before. The case may be made, therefore, that the preacher should have, at least, a Master's Degree. Consider what one of the greatest preachers had to say about such a matter. Martin Luther said: 'When I preach I regard neither doctors nor magistrates, of whom I have about forty in the congregation. I have all my eyes on the servant maids and the children. And if the learned men are not well pleased with what they hear, well, the door is open.'[2] We need to see men with gentle and meek hearts in pulpits today.

When we consider the biblical qualifications for holding office in the church we discover that they are not in fact professional qualifications at all, rather they are personal qualities. It is worth emphasising that these are qualities of character rather than qualifications and credentials. One might say a theological education would help. Of course it would but it must never be a prerequisite that prevents potential pastors from ministering, especially men who are gentle and meek. One can become overly reliant on the cognitive capacities rather than the power of the Holy Spirit. Of course a man must have a professional approach to his work and this is not to excuse a shoddy approach to preaching or to argue against ministerial preparation but to speak against the practice of 'professionalism' that takes no account of gentleness or meekness. The words of the psalmist seem particularly apt: 'Some trust in chariots and some in horses, but we trust in the name of the LORD our God' (Psalm 20:7).

Pastoral search committees need to be careful in framing advertisements and selection criteria. Setting such educational criteria as a prerequisite in occupational selection effectively debars a whole group of eligible (according to biblical standards) people. Let us not lose sight of those wonderful words in Zechariah: 'Not by might nor by power, but by my Spirit, says the LORD Almighty' (4:6). And we do well to remember that the spirit of Christ was meek and gentle.

It is not appropriate to criticise men who dedicate themselves to the formal training of others for ministry. They are to be commended not condemned! Nevertheless there is a danger that some theological seminaries are becoming occupational institutions engaged in a ritualised process of qualification-earning. There are many great seminaries and Bible colleges but some appear to be more like businesses engaged in the service sector. It is entirely right for a man to aspire to a high level of educational attainment and achieve a Master's degree but what is more important is that he would have an evident degree of the Master in his life. Let us, therefore, esteem those who manifest the fruit of the Spirit as worthy candidates for leadership. Meekness/gentleness should be at the top of our list of selection criteria.

Everybody seems to want a dynamic leader but meekness should have some merit in our estimation of a man's suitability for Christian leadership. Christ was gentle and therefore gentleness is Christlikeness. As such it is important and if we fail to acknowledge this we are doing ourselves a great disservice by depriving ourselves of godly leaders. Submitting to God's will is more important than many other qualities we cherish. Pride (the opposite of meekness) is an obstacle that keeps us from God's best. Let us begin to watch for signs of meekness in others and ourselves and let us renounce the way of the world by putting a premium on meekness.

The Meek Lamb

We have already seen that Jesus described himself as 'meek' (Matthew 11:29). He was the Lamb of God (John 1:29), the sacrifice who did not resist crucifixion because it was the divine will (Luke 22:42). Are you always demanding your own way? Do you have trouble getting along with others? Do you get angry when things don't go your way? Consider Christ, meditate on him and model him in the power of the Holy Spirit. The prophetic words of Isaiah concerning Christ give us some sense of just how gentle and meek Christ is: 'A bruised reed he will not break, and a smouldering wick he will not snuff out' (Isaiah 42:3). Matthew 12 tells us that Christ was the fulfilment of that prophecy. A bruised reed is a very fragile thing indeed it is difficult to handle without having it snap in two. Yet Christ can touch the most tender and vulnerable areas of our lives and not break us! What a Saviour! Are we a people who can come into contact with the weak and needy in our society and present them with the truth of the gospel in such a way that although they are convicted of their need of Christ yet they are not destroyed by that same truth?

Many Christians today are seeking the Lord in dramatic, earth-shattering experiences. There is no doubt that God can and sometimes does deal with people in the most extraordinary way. But God does not always or even often chose sensational means for our encounters with him. When Elijah, the prophet of God, fled from Jezebel in fear to a cave in Mount Horeb, the mountain of God, the Lord communicated with him in an unexpected way. Let us recall those amazing words in 1 Kings:

The LORD said, 'Go out and stand on the mountain in the presence of the LORD, for the LORD is about to pass by.' Then a great and powerful wind tore the mountains apart and shattered the rocks before the LORD, but the LORD was not in the wind. After the wind there was an earthquake, but the LORD was not in the earthquake. After the earthquake came a fire, but the LORD was not in the fire. And after the fire came a gentle whisper. When Elijah heard it, he pulled his cloak over his face and went out and stood at the mouth of the cave (19:11–13).

Where do we think we will encounter God? Are we looking for the spectacular and breathtaking rendezvous with the Almighty? This false expectation has driven some believers to desire what is novel and unconventional. The reality is that God is far more likely to speak to us in a whisper. When we are discouraged, afraid, feeling isolated and alone and when our perspective has become distorted, God draws alongside and whispers. The earth may shake and the winds may roar and the fire may be ablaze all around but God comes gently and meekly and whispers to us and then we know something of his true nature. He is the meek and marvellous one! O that we could be more like him in manifesting gentleness and meekness as evidence of the work of the Holy Spirit in our lives.

The teaching of Christ that the meek shall inherit the earth seems to run counter to the prevailing ethos of modern society, which teaches that we must be assertive if we are to be successful. But what is success? How can we define it? In the world's eyes success is defined in terms of achieving favourable outcomes in the accomplishment of particular aims. As such the attainment of wealth, fame or position is seen as success. However, as believers we would want to be concerned not only about outcomes but also the process of working toward certain objectives and especially the motives imbuing such processes. Christians should not be lacking in resolve and have a deserved reputation as feeble people. Believers should present an alternative to the aggression that seems to be esteemed as a virtue. Being gentle and meek may take great courage in our society.

Meekness not weakness

Meekness is confused with weakness. We have already alluded to the fact that we would not consider Moses (a meek man) to be a weak man, as he is rightly understood as one of the greatest heroes in the history of Israel. How many leadership-training programmes would hold Moses up as one from whom we may learn great lessons? When Miriam and Aaron spoke against Moses he did not become defensive or malicious (see Numbers 12). Rather he showed great restraint and maturity and such exemplary behaviour shows the strength of gentleness. Today's church needs leaders who are gentle. It is a quality that is very pleasing in God's sight. It is also a quality that is very attractive to those who are tired of the aggressive leadership principles of the business world.

The power of gentleness

There is a power in gentleness that is very attractive to people who are weary of warring their way in this world. Jesus demonstrated great gentleness despite opposition, criticism and plots to entrap him. His triumphal entry to Jerusalem tells us something of his meekness. He did not enter riding a chariot. There was no fanfare of trumpets. This was a different kind of regal procession. He entered riding on a donkey! He did not come as a politician with flattering words designed to increase his popularity. Even though the land of his birth was occupied by an imperial power he did not come as a military leader or liberator with sword and words designed to incite insurrection or popular uprising. This was no mock pageantry artificially contrived to entertain the crowd. This was the fulfilment of prophecy. That entry on a donkey conjures up a potent image of gentleness that is very powerful indeed. When he was arrested in the Garden of Gethsemane he did not resist or retaliate. This is not weakness, this is great strength exhibited in meekness and gentleness. Christ was focused on his mission to go to Calvary and no matter what Satan tried to fling at him Jesus remained undeterred from going to the cross. He could have fought and won but his mind was on the attainment of the higher goal and if we follow this example we will not get embroiled in petty battles, defending our reputations and winning arguments. Our thoughts like his should be focused on the ultimate glory of God. This is what it means to be gentle, humble and meek. Christ was gentle and his disciples, as learners who seek to be like their Master, must become like him. Every day presents opportunities for meekness and gentleness so let us, with the help of the Holy Spirit, seize those opportunities today.

Many people in Western society tend to think of gentleness as a failing, especially in men. Gentleness may be expected and admired in women but it is not a quality that is generally admired in men. A man who is gentle in this world is often seen as effeminate or smarmy and unctuous. If we are to be gentle people we need to feel secure in our faith and this confidence in Christ will enable us to weather storms with a gentle spirit. A gentle spirit will enable us to be constructive and compassionate at times when it is necessary to be critical of certain attitudes or actions in others. Our thinking needs to be re-orientated and be aligned with Scripture (Romans 12:2). A necessary first stage in becoming gentle is to desire this grace in our lives. If we admire it in others rather than despising it and if we pray for the strength to be gentle then God will honour the spiritual nature of that aspiration. He will help us to foster this fruit in our lives. Our humility, meekness and gentleness ought not to be an artificially contrived thing or merely a veneer that masks repressed aggression. People soon see through that kind of syrupy and ingratiating facade. Gentle actions come from gentle hearts just as apples grow on apple trees! In this we are seeking the heart of Christ, the gentle Saviour. If we have a meek attitude toward God we will also develop a gentle attitude in our human relationships. The reverse is equally true and therefore we can say that people who are aggressive and hostile in their human relationships have a haughty spirit in their relationship with the Lord.

The futility of fighting

The transformed believer will manifest gentleness with friends and foes alike and in doing so brings honour to God. When we come to the end of our own strength there we see the possibilities and power of gentleness. When we see the futility of fighting then we can leave behind the frustration and failure of the world's values and choose to be gentle. Gentleness is the hallmark of Christian maturity and those who desire to cultivate Christian character must realise that being gentle shows an awareness and appreciation of the believer's status in Christ. Only those who are secure in this knowledge will manifest the secure and stable gentleness of Christ. A gentle spirit gives us a degree of immunity to the whims of others and enables us to maintain a steady course in the storms of criticism.

We see the strength of gentleness in Jesus when he refused to defend himself against false accusations. Christ could have won his case by argument but he was secure in the Father's will. Gentleness is the appropriate approach to handling our frustrations. When we fail the Lord (as we are bound to do in our Christian walk) he does not berate us and banish us. The Holy Spirit gently brings conviction to our hearts and his voice is so gentle that it is a whisper. Anybody who has ever heard the voice of the Holy Spirit in this way will attest to the fact that it is absolutely compelling.

Peter tells wives that they ought to have 'a gentle and quiet spirit, which is of great worth in God's sight' (1 Peter 3:4). Here is clear statement about what God values. A 'gentle and quiet spirit' can be a very potent and compelling means of winning respect, not just for ourselves but for our God and his glorious gospel. A similar sentiment is expressed in a pithy manner in the book of Proverbs: 'Charm is deceptive, and beauty is fleeting; but a woman who fears the LORD is to be praised' (31:30). Peter is advocating an alternative means of seeking to persuade others that can be more powerful than argument. It is an elegant and eloquent way of engaging, not just the minds of others but their hearts also. This inward beauty is very attractive to the discerning Christian man who values the quality of Christian character above other superficial considerations. Any right thinking man would want to be in the company of such a woman because she will be a source of comfort and strength to him. The book of Proverbs speaks of the worth of a godly woman in these terms: 'A wife of noble character who can find? She is worth far more than rubies' (31:10). Solomon goes on to point out that, 'She is clothed with strength and dignity' (31:25). There is a saying that 'beauty is in the eye of the beholder' which means that it is a matter of subjective perception. For Christians, however, spiritual beauty is a matter of observing the objective criteria of God's Word and gentleness is held before us as an adornment that pleases God.

Notes on Chapter 8

1 The same applies to the belief that if we have more money at our disposal for the programmes of the church and/or more manpower that we will be more effective Christians. Education, money and manpower are wonderful but they do not, necessarily, make us more effective any more than their absence, necessarily, makes us less effective.

2 Quoted in **D. Martyn Lloyd Jones,** *Preaching and Preachers,* (London, Hodder & Stoughton, 1971), p.128.

Self-control

'The fruit of the Spirit is self-control …'

The Authorised Version translates this grace of God as 'temperance' but the New International Version renders it as 'self-control'. 'Temperance' means moderation, especially in eating and drinking. It is often understood as abstinence, especially total abstinence from alcohol. To be temperate means to avoid excess. This interpretation has some merit because it opposes drunkenness in the corresponding list of vices, which immediately precede the verses that list the fruit of the Spirit. However, 'self-control' has a broader meaning that includes 'temperance' and 'temperate'. The word used is *enkrateia*, which has a more comprehensive meaning than the word *néphalios*, which sometimes carries a restricted reference to drinking. Paul tells Timothy that in the last days people will lack self-control: 'But mark this: There will be terrible times in the last days. People will be … without self-control' (2 Timothy 3:1–5). A sign of the end times will be increasing self-indulgence without restraint. Selfishness will be prevalent. End times will therefore be marked by moral incontinence, and drunkenness is merely a symptom of that morally degenerate condition. Some societies have become so used to drunkenness that to hear it described in the terms above may seem ridiculous. Man's depravity will deepen and this process is well under way. We read about things in the newspaper that shock us and cause us distress. The reality of sin comes from the sinful nature of humanity.

Self under the control of the Holy Spirit

So when this verse in Galatians tells us that, 'the fruit of the Spirit is … self-control' we must not think of *the self in control* but *the self under the control of the Holy Spirit*. This is absolutely crucial to our understanding of this grace of God in the lives of those who are redeemed. Scripture tells us that the person without 'self-control' is a pitiful sight. Thus we read

'Like a city whose walls are broken down is a man who lacks self-control' (Proverbs 25:28). This verse conveys the idea of ruin and vulnerability. We have an image of a city that was once splendid but now that former glory has departed. Because its walls are in ruins it is susceptible to invasion and control by enemy forces.

Knowing right from wrong

Notions of *right* and *wrong* are becoming increasingly obsolete and the concepts of *loyalty* and *service* are deemed to be archaic and antiquated values that do not belong to this postmodern world. In a society where everything is permissible, promiscuity is merely symptomatic of a greater malady, namely sin. Sin ultimately manifests itself in selfishness. This is the way of the world but the Christian church is not to be a microcosm of the world, rather it is to be radically different.

The idea that the Christian should exercise self-control is not just a peculiar Pauline teaching. Peter in his second epistle also draws attention to the necessity for this grace in the life of the believer: 'make every effort to add to your faith goodness; and to goodness, knowledge; and to knowledge, self-control; and to self-control, perseverance; and to perseverance, godliness; and to godliness, brotherly kindness; and to brotherly kindness, love. For if you possess these qualities in increasing measure, they will keep you from being ineffective and unproductive in your knowledge of our Lord Jesus Christ' (1:5–8). In fact Peter tells us that these qualities (including self-control) make us effective and productive believers. The clear implication is that without such graces we will be ineffective and unproductive! I have never yet met a Christian who did not at least desire to be effective and productive. That is what the fruit of the Spirit is all about. It is the outworking of God's grace in the life of the believer, the result of the indwelling Spirit. We tend to think that if a Christian's life is ineffectual and impotent it is the result of feeble faith. The barren believer is fruitless because he has not sought diligently to see these other graces (including self-control) added to his faith. If we want to yield fruit for God's glory and if we want to produce what is profitable then we must take seriously the necessity of bearing these fruit of the Spirit. God is willing to bestow bounteous blessing on incompetent and incapable believers so that they become profitable and prolific people who yield a harvest of fruit for the Master.

As the world becomes increasingly darker we are to shine brighter! Self-control is about the power of the Holy Spirit controlling the behaviour, emotions, attitudes and actions of those who are Christ's disciples. We are all subject to temptations and we all have a propensity to lose our temper. I don't wish to be facetious but the person who claims to have complete control over his tongue should have it surgically removed, dipped in bronze and mounted on the mantle-piece before it can do any harm! In short the Christian who does not feel the need for greater self-control is a seriously deluded individual. The world needs to see a people who have control over temptation, temper and tongue. We might fall short of being the paragons of virtue that we ought to be but this is no excuse for not putting our house in order.

Not just concealing and controlling emotions

Some people are good at concealing their emotions and others are good at controlling their behaviour to conform to the conventions of society. But 'self-control' as fruit of the Spirit is not merely about concealing attitudes and controlling behaviour to conform to the expectations of others. Rather self-control is essentially about 'the self' coming under the control of the Holy Spirit. The self is the sinful fallen nature of man. This is the nub of the matter. It is not, therefore, about 'the self' being in control. Most (if not all) of the problems of mankind spring from a desire of the self to be in control. The egocentric nature of sinful man wants to satisfy its appetite for self-indulgence and gratify every inclination of a wicked heart. The 'self' demands its own way and desires to be master of its own destiny. The self must have power and possessions. Self must satisfy every lust of the flesh. We, as believers, certainly do not want the self to be in control; rather we desire that the self come under the divine control of the Holy Spirit.

We were once slaves to the sinful desires of the 'self' and we bore the fruit of this in all our wrongdoing in thought, word and deed. Paul in his letter to the Romans reminds them that whereas they were once controlled by their sinful nature and bore fruit accordingly they are now under the control of the Spirit and ought, therefore, to bear fruit in keeping with that new nature. Thus we read:

Chapter 9

So, my brothers, you also died to the law through the body of Christ, that you might belong to another, to him who was raised from the dead, in order that we might bear fruit to God. For when we were controlled by the sinful nature, the sinful passions aroused by the law were at work in our bodies, so that we bore fruit for death. But now, by dying to what once bound us, we have been released from the law so that we serve in the new way of the Spirit, and not in the old way of the written code. (Romans 7:4–6).

What Paul is saying essentially is that the believer comes under new management. Self-control as fruit of the Spirit is therefore about conforming to the expectations of God. Have you ever seen a restaurant that is run down and the quality of the food is poor and then the business is bought as a going concern? The new management renovates the premises and recruits a new chef. Then the new owner puts a sign in the window saying 'UNDER NEW MANAGEMENT'. That is what conversion is about: the self under new management. A great improvement should be evident.

When we depend on our own strength and inner resources we are bound to fail. It is certainly true that some people have greater willpower than others and much may be achieved with determination. But the believer is not deceived about the limitations of human resolve and tenacity even though the world teaches that we have untapped and unlimited power within. How often have your resolutions failed and how many regrets do you harbour because of your lack of resolve? The reality is that good intentions often end in failure. But important areas of our lives, especially with regard to our temptations, our tempers and the use of our tongues ought not to be out of control.

Confidence in Christ

Why do we fail when we decide to never say certain things or do certain things again? Why does that serious intention flounder? Why does the tongue seem to have a mind of its own? The primary reason for lack of self-control is a misplaced confidence in our own ability to master our wills and passions. Self-confidence deceives us and deprives us of success. Our wills and passions must come under the auspices and good government of the Holy Spirit. Thus we need to exchange our self-confidence for faith in the Spirit's power to control. We cannot achieve self-control merely because we are Christians. It is only when we learn to submit our self-confidence to the power of God that we begin to experience 'self-control'; that is the self under the control of the Holy Spirit. Then we can truly say: 'I can do everything through him who gives me strength' (Philippians 4:13).

I have no desire to discourage believers by disparaging 'determination' and divesting 'willpower' of its potency to produce results. There is a plus and minus side to self-confidence and when we consider the positives we must admit that 'self confidence' enables us to achieve some things. Nevertheless on the negative side we must say that in the spiritual realm self-confidence limits us to the restricted capacity of human potential alone. The Holy Spirit adds a divine dimension in this area. Man in his natural, unconverted state has neither the inclination nor the ability to imitate Christ and cannot manifest the fruit of the Spirit. The fruit of the Spirit is the outcome of a life possessed by the Spirit of God! Thus Christ said:

Watch out for false prophets. They come to you in sheep's clothing, but inwardly they are ferocious wolves. By their fruit you will recognize them. Do people pick grapes from thorn bushes, or figs from thistles? Likewise every good tree bears good fruit, but a bad tree bears bad fruit. A good tree cannot bear bad fruit, and a bad tree cannot bear good fruit. Every tree that does not bear good fruit is cut down and thrown into the fire. Thus, by their fruit you will recognize them. Not everyone who says to me, 'Lord, Lord,' will enter the kingdom of heaven, but only he who does the will of my Father who is in heaven. Many will say to me on that day, 'Lord, Lord, did we not prophesy in your name and in your name drive out demons and perform many miracles?' Then I will tell them plainly, 'I never knew you: away from me, you evildoers!' (Matthew 7:15–23).

In these words Jesus is saying that prophesying, exorcisms and spectacular miracles performed in his name is not necessarily evidence of true discipleship. He says that just as thorn bushes and thistles cannot yield grapes and figs respectively, neither can those who are not born of the Spirit manifest fruit that comes from the Spirit of God. Not only that, but Jesus gives us some advice on how to discern the difference between those who belong to him and those who do not when he says: 'By their fruit you will recognize them' (v. 16). The fruit reveals who we are! Only those who are connected to Christ can produce fruit that pleases God.

Thus we may read of incidents in Scripture where that divine dimension is evident. Joshua, for example, leading the people of Israel to victory at Jericho shows us a man who is supremely confident, not in himself or the ability of the army he commands, but in his God! Consider the youthful David defeating the Goliath of the Philistine army. Armed not just with a slingshot but with a passion for the reputation of God and complete trust in the power of that God, he saw the enemy delivered into his hands and destroyed. Let us recall Luke's historical account in Acts of how, in the power of the Holy Spirit, the unlearned disciples of Christ were used to turn the world upside down. Do we want to see the strongholds of the enemy crumble? Do we want to see those giants that oppose us felled? Do we want to be instrumental in seeing God's great project of redemption prospering?

Abandoning self-confidence

Then let us abandon self-confidence for the control of the Holy Spirit, which is the true meaning of 'self-control'. Then we will see defeat changed to victory in God's power. So let us exchange our willpower for God's power; then we will know that we can do whatever it is that has been defeating us and we will also know that it is only through his power that we succeed. If our confidence is in Christ then we will be able to say, 'I can' instead of merely, 'I want to'. If we have been trying to win with willpower we will soon learn that our power is limited. God's power, however, is unlimited. When God's unlimited power is operative within us we are equipped to win.

So in the area of self-control we need to substitute faith for self-confidence. We need to see our willpower converted into confidence in God's power. We need to see our weakness replaced with God's strength. When we fail (as we inevitably do) we need to know that we can exchange our guilt for God's forgiveness. Remorse over habitual failures of the past may result in discouragement where we become de-motivated and abandon hope of victory. We are designed to feel guilty when we sin and offend God but we must always remember that God forgives the guilty who confess their sin (1 John 1:9).

The fruit of the Spirit will change our lives if we yield to his complete control. We must remind ourselves that it is the root of the plant that leads to the fruit of the plant. Thus: abiding in Christ means being guided and governed by the Spirit of God. There is no place for hypocrisy. Christ condemned those who presented favourably in external matters of religious observance but were corrupt on the inside. Let us recall the words of Jesus on this issue: 'Woe to you, teachers of the law and Pharisees, you hypocrites! You clean the outside of the cup and dish, but inside they are full of greed and self-indulgence. Blind Pharisee! First clean the inside of the cup and dish, and then the outside also will be clean' (Matthew 23:25–26). Christ often expressed contempt for hypocrisy but in this passage he reveals that 'self-indulgence' is at the core of a people who pretend to speak on his behalf. May we who profess to be disciples of Christ never warrant such condemnation from his lips! Self-control is the opposite of self-indulgence because the self is subordinate to the will of the Holy Spirit.

In your anger do not sin

Before we conclude our exploration of the meaning and application of self-control there is one incident in the gospels that requires our attention: let us recall that occasion when Christ made a whip and drove people out from the temple courts

When it was almost time for the Jewish Passover, Jesus went up to Jerusalem. In the temple courts he found men selling cattle, sheep and doves, and others sitting at tables exchanging money. So he made a whip out of cords, and drove all from the temple area, both sheep and cattle; he scattered the coins of the money changers and overturned their tables. To those who sold doves he said, 'Get these out of here! How dare you turn my Father's house into a market!' (John 2: 13–16).

Was this an occasion when Jesus lost his temper and lashed out at those who were using the house of God for inappropriate activity? Is this an incident where Christ is out of control? Is it to be understood as a regrettable intemperate outburst? The answer to these questions is a resounding no! There was no sin in the Saviour. John puts the incident in context for us: 'His disciples remembered that it is written: "Zeal for your house will consume me"' (John 2:17). Here is holy anger, a righteous indignation at an outrageous violation of the truth entrusted to his chosen people. Jesus is concerned only for the honour and glory of God. He had the authority to expel these merchants who were damaging the reputation of God. Scripture does not teach that anger itself is necessarily sinful. It is the way we deal with that anger that may be sinful. Paul counselled the Ephesian believers, 'In your anger do not sin' (4:26).

A day of greater righteous indignation is approaching and those who are not true disciples of Jesus will be driven away. Teaching on Hell has fallen into abeyance in some circles but it will be a future reality. It is important to say in relation to this that Hell will not be the vindictive act of a malicious God but rather it will be divine justice. Just as Jesus did no wrong when he drove people from the temple on that occasion recorded in the gospel so too the final judgement will not be intemperate, irrational or in any way inappropriate. God has the authority to judge and punish. Let us never forget that Jesus is the supreme example of self-control and this is evident in how he endured betrayal, arrest, false trial and crucifixion.

Thought, temper, tongue and temptation

The Christian should enjoy liberty from the bondage of religious systems that emphasise observance of the law as a means of salvation. It is all too easy for those converted from such oppressive structures to gradually develop another order that is essentially legalistic. On the other hand a radical rejection of rules and constraints leads to licentiousness which is an abuse of grace and true liberty in the Lord. A proper celebration of our liberty demands self-control. Self-control for the believer is submission to the divine will. Christ prayed in the Garden of Gethsemane: 'not my will, but yours be done' (Luke 22:42). This is a prayer that was uttered at a time of great anguish. This is what self control is about, the submission of our wills to the will of God so that his glorious purposes may be fulfilled in us. As Paul told the Philippians: 'Your attitude should be the same as that of Christ Jesus' (Philippians 2:5). Although every Christian must make an effort to control thought, temper, tongue, temptation and so on there is a sense in which self-control is not really about self-management. We all struggle with temptations and there is a great need for self-control in a world where people feel justified in gratifying every sinful lust of the flesh. The honest and self-aware Christian will know that there are areas of life where greater self-control is needed. Bringing this before the Lord in regular prayer and yielding to the control of the Spirit will enable us to produce this fruit. The Christian is engaged in a very real spiritual struggle where the natural inclination of the heart is pulling in one direction and the Holy Spirit is urging in another. Christian maturity is essentially about coming more and more under the influence of the Spirit so that the inclination of our hearts is to please him rather than our own selfish desires. Nevertheless we should realise that coming under the efficacious influence of the Holy Spirit will ultimately be pleasing to us as well because his will is: 'good, pleasing and perfect' (Romans 12:2).

Cameos concerning control

The life of David provides us with some very interesting cameos regarding this matter of self-control. In 1 Samuel 24–26 we read the accounts of how David resisted the temptation to kill Saul. Even though he had justifiable cause and opportunity to kill the man who was seeking to kill him, David exercised restraint and spared the life of Saul in a cave in En Gedi and again in Saul's tent on the hill of Hakilah. Then in 2 Samuel 11 we read the tragic story of David's failure to exercise self-control and how he yielded to temptation, committed adultery with Bathsheba and commissioned the murder of her husband Uriah. We learn from these incidents that on the occasions when he exercised self-control he was focused on the sovereign will of God and conscious that, in spite of being hunted, Saul was still the Lord's anointed king. Thus we read in 1 Samuel 24: 'The LORD forbid that I should do such a thing to my master, the LORD's anointed, or lift my hand against him; for he is the anointed of the LORD' (v. 6). This thinking is developed more fully in a later chapter:

Abishai said to David, 'Today God has given your enemy into your hands. Now let me pin him to the ground with one thrust of my spear; I won't strike him twice.' But David said to Abishai, 'Don't destroy him! Who can lay a hand on the LORD's anointed and be guiltless? As surely as the LORD lives,' he said, 'the LORD himself will strike him;

either his time will come and he will die, or he will go into battle and perish. But the LORD forbid that I should lay a hand on the LORD's anointed' (26:8–11).

I have no doubt that David could have convinced himself and persuaded others that killing Saul was the right thing to do but he chose rather to exercise self-control in the face of great provocation. In the case of Bathsheba David chose self-gratification rather than self-control. On that occasion he was not focused on the will of the Lord but on his own wicked will. The results of that shift of focus were disastrous. Kings in Israel were anointed with oil as a sign that they were chosen and commissioned by God. David's refusal to kill Saul demonstrates his respect for the authority of the office even when the person holding that office does not merit such respect. There is a godly principle inherent in this attitude and we would do well to observe it.

Finding grace to help us in our time of need

Our attitude to the divine will is central in determining the outcome in times of temptation. Knowing that God will graciously supply the strength we need if we turn to him in our struggles gives us the confidence that enables us to exercise self-control. What a comfort it is to know that Christ is our caring companion. As the writer to the Hebrews says: 'For we do not have a high priest who is unable to sympathise with our weaknesses, but we have one who has been tempted in every way, just as we are—yet was without sin. Let us then approach the throne of grace with confidence, so that we may receive mercy and find grace to help us in our time of need' (Hebrews 4:15–16).

Real emancipation

Self-control is the final grace listed in the fruit of the Spirit. It is set in stark contrast to the 'acts of the sinful nature' listed in Galatians 5:19–21. By juxtaposing these vices and virtues Paul is emphasising the profound dissimilarity between these things. The list of vices refers to such sinful activity as sexual immorality, impurity, debauchery, hatred, discord, jealousy, fits of rage, selfish ambition, dissensions, factions, envy, drunkenness and orgies. Such things are entirely opposite to self-control and they indicate the kind of lifestyle likely to take hold of people who are not under the control of the Holy Spirit.

The contemporary consensus is that the notion of self-control advocated by Christians is a religious tactic for repressing people. Today's philosophy says do whatever you feel like doing. This is seen as a moral emancipation whereby the constraints imposed by Christians are cast off so that liberty may be fully enjoyed. On closer inspection however we find that those who revel in excess without inhibition frequently find themselves trapped in destructive lifestyles. The lure of such a philosophy may be likened to the attraction a moth may have for the fatal flames of a campfire.

A fatal flaw

Leaders who lack self-control ultimately reveal their weakness and unsuitability for such office. Consider Adolf Hitler. One could not deny that he was a charismatic leader, powerful orator, skilled military tactician and astute politician. Nevertheless his strengths knew no moral restraint and history has rightly relegated him to take his place in the chronicles of the twentieth century as an evil despot. The same could be said of the Roman Emperor Nero. He had absolute power but was also absolutely corrupt and profoundly cruel. These men knew nothing of self-control. They show us where power and authority without self-control may take us. Consider the sailor who harnesses the potentially destructive power of the wind to navigate his route to his desired destination. That is what our lives are like. Self-control is like the sails that harness the wind and convert it into energy. If those sails are not hoisted and used with purpose the vessel is in serious danger of being blown off course or worse.

Developing a code of conduct

Self-control is about having opportunity to do wrong but not succumbing to it. A father may be able to control his children while they are at a young age and ensure that they do not engage in certain undesirable behaviour. The child may conform to the father's expectations because he is either deprived of opportunity to indulge his desires or because he knows that certain punishment will result from his deviant action. This however is not self-control on the part of the child but rather paternal control in spite of the child's desires. If on the other hand the father teaches the child to understand and appreciate the difference between right and wrong, and the child develops an internal and personal code of ethics that corresponds to the father's moral standards and behaves in accordance with that code, he is then exercising self-control.

This is how it ought to be with the heavenly Father and his Christian child. God wants to instil virtue in us rather than have us begrudgingly conform to standards that we do not really believe in. In doing this we come to that place of self-control that is ultimately established on the basis of the Spirits paternal and loving control. This is the kind of discipline the Lord uses with his children. It is not merely punitive. Our heavenly Father desires to put us in control of ourselves so that we can make biblically informed and therefore wise moral choices. God wants his children to develop those critical abilities that enable them to live harmoniously with the consequences of their actions. Ultimately the believer has a choice. He can obey his base instincts or he can obey the Holy Spirit. The former destroys the potential we have in Christ whereas the latter employs us as disciples of the Master. God gradually releases responsibility to those who yield to him. He allows us to take charge of our own lives as we mature.

The Holy Spirit is sovereign

Self-control is not about self-sovereignty but Spirit-sovereignty and that involves self-surrender to God's control. It is when we submit to the good government of God that we come to understand the true meaning of self-control, which may be defined as the self under the control of the Holy Spirit. In his letter to the Ephesians Paul says: 'Do not get drunk on wine, which leads to debauchery. Instead, be filled with the Spirit' (5:18). If you have ever observed a person who is drunk you will notice that his speech is slurred and he staggers about unsteadily. Such a person has lost the conventional level of inhibition that is normal in societal relationships. In other words his words, walk and general mental state come under the dominant influence of alcohol, it masters him and controls him. There is a force at work in his bloodstream that overpowers him. He has willingly imbibed in order to get himself into such a condition. The parallel for the Christian is that we ought to come under the compelling influence of the person of the Holy Spirit so much so that our spiritual walk and spiritual talk are obviously under his sway. We can choose to allow that greater force to dominate our lives.

The Holy Spirit is the person who should have control or ownership of our lives. Seeking to be masterful in our own strength with regard to our passions is never going to produce the fruit of the Spirit in our lives. Nevertheless, there is a sense in which self-control is a discipline that is learned by making right choices. People learn certain patterns of behaviour by making choices. Choices informed by Scripture and sensitive to the prompting of the Holy Spirit through a quickened conscience, promotes positive outcomes.

On the other hand poor principles promote negative results. The reality is that if we do not learn to control our passions they will control us. This is particularly evident in the self-indulgent sexual behaviour of our generation. The training of character by promoting self-discipline is not part of the world's way of addressing the problem of pre-marital or extra-marital sex. The world thinks that such an idea is laughable rather than laudable. It needs to see a people who take God seriously in their lifestyles.

Helpful not harmful habits

Self-control is about having helpful rather than harmful habits because even good things when taken to excess may become gross indulgences without self-control. Those who lack self-control habitually follow their feelings. Lack of self-control is about pleasing self whereas self-control is about pleasing Christ. We live in a world where we have become accustomed to the idea of instant gratification. We have instant food, instant credit, and instant access to information. It is easy in such a world to indulge our urges. We can be driven by our own whims and fancies or alternatively led by the Spirit of God. The apostle Paul wrote to the Galatians: 'live by the Spirit, and you will not gratify the desires of the sinful nature' (Galatians 5:16). Living by the Spirit means being born of the Spirit and having our consciences quickened by his power. Living by the Spirit, means regularly listening to God's voice by reading Scripture. In today's world people-centred approaches promote a philosophy of empowerment through education and access to a host of services. The reality is that people are never fully empowered unless they come under the loving influence of the Holy Spirit. True self-control is a supernatural rather than a natural thing and success will first mean accepting the failure of self-government and yielding to God's government in our lives. Bearing the fruit of the Spirit comes from being rooted in God. Thus we read in Jeremiah: 'blessed is the man who trusts in the LORD, whose confidence is in him. He will be like a tree planted by the water that sends out its roots by the stream. It does not fear when heat comes; its leaves are always green. It has no worries in a year of drought and never fails to bear fruit' (Jeremiah 17:7–8).

Commencing and continuing by grace

We came to faith by the grace of God and we must continue that walk of faith by God's grace. We are urged to 'live by the Spirit' and to 'walk by the Spirit' and these exhortations indicate that our active participation is required in order to conform to God's expectations. Being led by the Spirit involves our choosing to follow the Spirit's leading. As Christians we bear the noble name of Christ so let us honour him in thought, word and deed. Let us live out the thought expressed in Isaiah: 'your name and renown are the desire of our hearts' (26:8b). May God grant us the grace we need to manifest the fruit of the Spirit for our good and God's glory!

Study guide

Chapter 1: Love

1. Read Galatians 5:16–26 and discuss the difference between life in the Spirit and life in the flesh.
2. How does life in the Spirit start?
3. What is love? Make a serious attempt to describe and define it. Where do we get our definition of love? How does the Christian understanding of love differ to the world's view?
4. In what way is the fruit of the Spirit different to the gifts of the Spirit? Read 1 Corinthians 12 and compare this passage with Galatians 5:22–23.
5. Discuss the love of God as displayed in the life and death of Jesus. What principles do we find in his love (e.g. compassion, sacrifice …) and how do we apply these principles at home, church and workplace?
6. What does love for God mean? Read Matthew 22:34–40 and discuss the implications of this passage. Talk about Christian love in relation to God, his church and those outside the church.

Chapter 2: Joy

1. Read Psalm 126. What is the source and nature of true joy?
2. Joy is the natural outcome of the Holy Spirit's activity. We see this in Acts 13:52. How should this influence the mood in our times of worship and fellowship?
3. Read Psalm 51:12 and discuss what can hinder joy in the life of the believer.
4. What does Jesus say about the quality of life we should have (John 10:10)? Discuss the past, present and future dimensions of our joy in Christ.
5. The apostle Paul spoke of the believers at Thessalonica as a source of joy to him (See 1 Thessalonians 2:19). He revelled in them as a father might take keen delight in his children. This was a church that God graciously started through the ministry of Paul (see Acts 16:1–9). In this we see how his heart was in harmony with heaven (see Luke 15:10). What do we learn from this about evangelism?

6. Read John 15:5–11. What does this passage have to say about joy and how to attain it and maintain it?

Chapter 3: Peace

1. If peace is a universal hope why is it so difficult to achieve it? Answer with particular reference to Romans 3:23 and Romans 5:1.
2. There is restlessness in the human soul that can only be stilled by God Read Isaiah 57:19–21 and discuss the cause and cure for that condition.
3. What is meant by 'generation', 'degeneration' and 'regeneration'? Discuss this in relation to 'spiritual disorder' as the human condition and the need for the restoration of spiritual order.
4. Read Romans 5:6–9 and Ephesians 2:13–17 what do these verses tell us about the source of peace and the route to peace?
5. Romans 12:18–19 speaks clearly about our responsibility to live peaceably. Consider the implications of this in our personal relationships, at home, in church, at college and in the workplace. What light does Colossians 3:15 shed on this?
6. Read Philippians 4:6–7 In the light of these verses explain why the peace that comes from knowing Christ as Saviour and Lord transcends all understanding.

Chapter 4: Patience

1. God's patience is an expression of his love because it permits opportunity for repentance, restitution and restoration. A real understanding and appreciation of God's patience can help us to be patient with others. Patience involves a willingness to forgive. Even when people repeatedly hurt us we are called to habitually forgive. Discuss this in relation to the parable of the unmerciful servant (Matthew 18:21–35).
2. How does the cross put patience in proper perspective?
3. From your reading of the chapter on *Patience* what is your understanding of 'biblical patience'?
4. Every human relationship needs patience and perhaps none more so than marriage. Consider the words of Paul and Peter respectively in

Colossians 3:19 and 1 Peter 3:7. What advice is given in these verses to husbands? Talk about the fact that God ignores the prayers of impatient husbands.

5. Read Proverbs 19:11. Patience comes from wisdom and maturity and it lends a dignity to the one who exercises it. When we have that heavenly perspective where we can detach ourselves from the difficulties that would otherwise tend to arouse impatience, then it is not just a mark of honour to us but a glory to the Holy Spirit who produces such fruit in the life of the believer. Discuss and give some examples of occasions where it is wise to overlook a fault and times when it would be unwise to do so.

6. When Christ hung on the cross and was humiliated and taunted he exercised astonishing patience. He could have called on the angels of heaven to take him down from the cross and avenge his tormentors. Yet he spoke to his Father in heaven and said: 'Father, forgive them, for they do not know what they are doing' (Luke 23:34). This provides great insight into the nature of God. Consider this attribute of God. (See 2 Peter 3:9; Exodus 34:6; Numbers 14:18; Nehemiah 9:17; Psalm 86:15; Psalm 103:8; Psalm 145:8; Joel 2:13; Jonah 4:2; Nahum 1:3). What does it mean for us?

Chapter 5: Kindness

1. Read 2 Samuel 9:1–13. List the ways that this passage illustrates God's kindness to us. Consider, for example the power, presence and provision of the king and talk about what this means for believers. Show how this passage relates to Ephesians 1:3–6.

2. There is more than just a present dimension to the kindness of God; there is also a future aspect to his kindness. Discuss the future dimension (See Ephesians 2:6–7).

3. With regard to the practical outworking of kindness as fruit of the Spirit we should take heed of Paul's instruction to the Colossians to clothe themselves with kindness (Colossians 3:12). What does this mean? How can we consciously and actively do this?

4. Titus 3:4 says: 'But when the kindness and love of God our Saviour appeared'. Here we learn that kindness is a quality of God's character.

Christ is kindness incarnate! His miracles were acts of kindness. The gospels are rich in accounts of his kindness to others: the undeserving, outsiders, the rejected and so on. Look up such incidents in the gospels and discuss how we can be instruments of kindness in a hurting world.

5. Consider the parable of the Good Samaritan (Luke 10:30–35). In this we see that kindness is central to true religion. What application can you see in this for today?

6. Paul tells us that 'love is kind' (1 Corinthians 13:4). If we profess to love others can we fail to show kindness?

Chapter 6: Goodness

1. Why do we need the power of the Holy Spirit to be good?

2. With regard to doing good we have stated that motivation is very important. Many people are part of religious systems where it is believed that doing good has value in terms of earning salvation. In the Bible, however, we learn that good works or observance of religious rites and rituals cannot earn salvation (See Ephesians 2:8–10). What is the appropriate Christian approach to good works?

3. Read aloud the following passage from the chapter on 'Goodness' and discuss it thoroughly:

'How can we know what is good and acceptable to God? There is no moral consensus in the world today and even Christians may be divided on what is right and what is wrong. We live in an age very much like that of the time spoken of in Judges where it says: 'every man did that which was right in his own eyes' (17:6, AV). The only way of knowing what is good and what is evil is to allow the Word of God to guide and govern us in all matters of faith and practice. It must regulate our religion and our reasoning about issues we face in society. The natural inclination of man's heart is toward wickedness. Thus Jeremiah writes: 'The heart is deceitful above all things' (17:9). We cannot and we dare not trust our own judgement. Our discernment must be rooted in the counsel of his infallible, inerrant, authoritative and efficacious Word. Proverbs cautions us about following the inclinations of our hearts rather than the mind of God: 'There is a way that seems right to a man, but in the end it leads to death' (14:12). We cannot be moral chameleons who adapt to whatever environment or culture we inhabit. The only situational ethics we can legitimately speak of is ethics situated in Scriptural principles! It is not easy to be good in a bad world. Our thinking may become warped in this world and that is one reason why we need the Word of God as it helps us to keep eternal perspective in earthly circumstances. We live in a pluralist society where the very concept of objective, absolute truth is perceived not just as antiquated but absurd. Epistemological and ethical fragmentation has led to moral relativism. All that relativism has to offer is ruin and eternal regret. In this context the only compass we have is the Word of God. Age-old Christian values that have held the fabric of society together are discarded and we might well ask with the psalmist: 'When the foundations are being destroyed, what can the righteous do?' (Psalm 11:3). We must help others to see that God is good and that his Word is good and wise and wonderful!'

4. Everybody is born in sin and has an innate tendency for wrongdoing and a propensity for evil. Paul tells us, 'all have sinned and fall short of the glory of God' (Romans 3:23). David said, 'Surely I was sinful at birth, sinful from the time my mother conceived me' (Psalm 51:5). Discuss this Scriptural position in relation to the optimism of humanism that believes people are inherently good.

5. Our election to salvation is God's choice. When was this choice made and on what basis? (See John 15:16; Acts 13:48; Romans 8:29–30; Ephesians 1:4–6, 11: 2 Thessalonians 2:13).

6. How does an understanding that our election to salvation is something 'unconditional' assist our worship of God? How does it stimulate holiness in living? How does it inform and motivate our evangelism?

Chapter 7: Faithfulness

1. In the 'Parable of the Talents' (Matthew 25:14–23) we see that those who are productive are commended for their faithfulness. Faithfulness is more than being custodians of what is entrusted to us. Christians are not just guardians of the truth. Christ's servants have an obligation to see the truth invested in others and producing fruit. What does this

mean in the reality of our daily lives? How do we go about doing this?

2. Read aloud the following passage from the chapter on 'Faithfulness'.

   'Being faithful in itself is not necessarily a good thing. We know from history, experience and common sense that many people manifest faithfulness to destructive ideologies, wrong causes and false religions. They may be exemplary in their faithfulness and yet misguided in adhering to the object of their loyalty. What does it mean to be faithful? If, as we have stated, God is faithful, then it may be helpful for us to understand what that means. God is faithful to himself. He is faithful to his Word. He is faithful to his love. He is faithful to his mercy. He is faithful to his justice and judgement. He keeps his covenant promises. God promises to redeem those who trust him for salvation. He will be faithful to that promise. God promises to condemn those who reject the gospel. He will be faithful to that promise. God follows through to fulfil what he desires and intends.'

   Why is it important to clarify that faithfulness is not necessarily an acceptable virtue? What are the implications of a proper understanding of 'acceptable faithfulness'? Consider, for example, evangelising not just the 'un-churched' but people who are faithful to false religious systems.

3. When we hear missionary reports from distant lands we are encouraged by the faithfulness of our brethren to the truth of God's Word. In this regard our hearts are in harmony with John (see 3 John 3). Christ was faithful to the truth of the Word despite hostility, ridicule and rejection. Consider the implications of imitating Christ especially in an age of inter-faith and ecumenical endeavour.

4. The Christian hope rests on God's faithfulness (see Lamentations 3:19–24). In the light of our failings why are these verses a comfort to believers?

5. In the spiritual realm it is difficult to quantify or measure success. According to the world's standards many people who have laboured faithfully without seeing much or even any positive results are deemed to be failures. The church must take great care to counter such business criteria being applied in evaluating Christian endeavour. Faithfulness is what counts in God's estimation. Faithfulness will be blessed. Thus we read in Matthew: 'It will be

good for that servant whose master finds him doing so when he returns' (24:46). Discuss the importance of faithfulness in a results/success driven world.

6. Read 1 Kings 22:1–38 and talk about the importance of ministerial faithfulness in today's world. Take time to pray for your pastor/minister.

Chapter 8: Gentleness

1. In 2 Corinthians 10:1 Paul appeals to the Corinthian church on the basis of Christ's gentleness. Is such an appeal relevant today?

2. What do you understand about gentleness from reading John 18:10–11? Consider your answer in the light of Matthew 11:29.

3. As we consider gentleness as fruit of the Spirit it is helpful for us to remember the relationship between the Holy Spirit and the believer. It is the Holy Spirit who brings about that conviction of sin whereby we become aware of our need of the saving grace of God. On conversion the Holy Spirit enters the believer and we ought to bear this in mind. Paul asks the question of believers: 'Do you not know that your body is a temple of the Holy Spirit, who is in you, whom you have received from God?' (1 Corinthians 6:19). How does gentleness honour God? How does its absence dishonour him?

4. Peter tells wives that they ought to have 'a gentle and quiet spirit, which is of great worth in God's sight' (1 Peter 3:4). Here is a clear statement about what God values. A 'gentle and quiet spirit' can be a very potent and compelling means of winning respect, not just for ourselves but for our God and his glorious gospel. Discuss the place of gentleness in our lifestyles and the power of gentleness in persuading others of the truth of the gospel. Consider that meekness is the mode of communication commended to the believer when responding to the inquiring or arguing non-Christian (1 Peter 3:15).

5. Why does the church need meek learners and meek leaders?

6. In 1 Samuel 16:1–13 we read the account of the choosing and anointing of David, who in appearance was the least likely candidate for office. What does this tell us about the necessity to look for spiritual qualities in candidates for leadership roles?

Chapter 9: Self-control

1. Paul tells Timothy that in the last days people will lack self-control (2 Timothy 3:1–5). A sign of the end times will be increasing self-indulgence without restraint. Selfishness will be prevalent. In what ways can the people of God be radically different?

2. Self-control for the believer is submission to the divine will. Christ prayed in the Garden of Gethsemane: 'not my will, but yours be done' (Luke 22:42). This is what self control is about, the submission of our wills to the will of God so that his glorious purposes may be fulfilled in us. As Paul told the Philippians: 'Your attitude should be the same as that of Christ Jesus' (Philippians 2:5). In what areas of our lives are we neglecting to submit to the will of God?

3. Although every Christian must make an effort to control thought, temper, tongue, temptation and so on, there is a sense in which self-control is not really about self-management. We all struggle with temptations and there is a great need for self-control in a world where people feel justified in gratifying every sinful lust of the flesh. The honest and self-aware Christian will know that there are areas of life where greater self-control is needed. How can we succeed in producing this fruit? Where do we start and how do we keep going?

4. 1 Samuel 24–26 we read the accounts of how David resisted the temptation to kill Saul. Even though he had justifiable cause and opportunity to kill the man who was seeking to kill him, David exercised restraint and spared the life of Saul in a cave in En Gedi and again in Saul's tent on the hill of Hakilah. Then in 2 Samuel 11 we read the tragic story of David's failure to exercise self-control and how he yielded to temptation, committed adultery with Bathsheba and commissioned the murder of her husband Uriah. What do we learn for our benefit from these cameos concerning self-control?

5. Read Hebrews 4:15–16. How do these verses help to bring comfort and confidence in times when we are struggling with self-control?

6. True self-control is a supernatural rather than a natural thing and success will first mean accepting the failure of self-government and yielding to God's government in our lives. Bearing the fruit of the

Spirit comes from being rooted in God. Read Jeremiah 17:7–8. Talk about the relationship between the root and the fruit.

Select bibliography

Kenneth L. Barker, & John Kohlenberger III, consulting editors, *NIV Bible Commentary: An Abridgement of The Expositor's Bible Commentary Volume 2: New Testament* (Grand Rapids: Zondervan, 1994; Published in Great Britain by Hodder & Stoughton).

John Blanchard, *More Gathered Gold: a treasury of quotations for Christians* (Welwyn: Evangelical Press,1986).

Stuart Briscoe, *The Fruit Of The Spirit: Growing in Christian Character. A Fisherman Bible Study Guide* (Colorado Springs: WaterBrook Press, 1994).

F.F. Bruce, *The Epistle to the Galatians, The New International Greek Testament Commentary* (Grand Rapids: Eerdmans, 1982).

R. Alan Cole, *Galatians* (Revised edition), Tyndale New Testament Commentaries (Leicester: Inter-Varsity Press, 1989).

J.D. Douglas, (organizing editor), et al. *The New Bible Dictionary* (Leicester: Tyndale Press, second edition, 1982).

Gordon Fee, *God's Empowering Presence* (Peabody MA, Hendrikson, 1994).

Sinclair B. Ferguson, David F. Wright. Consulting editor: **J.I. Packer,** *New Dictionary of Theology* (Leicester: Inter-Varsity Press, 1988).

Ron Hembree, *Fruit of the Spirit: The Keys To A Christian Personality* (Grand Rapids: Baker Books, 1969).

William Hendriksen, *New Testament Commentary: Galatians & Ephesians* (London: Banner of Truth Trust, 1968).

Matthew Henry, *Matthew Henry's Commentary On The Whole Bible: Complete and Unabridged in One Volume* (Peabody MA: Hendriksen Publishers, 1991).

D. Martyn Lloyd Jones, *Preaching and Preachers* (London: Hodder & Stoughton, 1971).

Select bibliography

Martin Luther King, *Strength to Love* (London: Collins Fount Paperback, 1977)

John R. Kohlenberger III, *The Interlinear NIV Hebrew-English Old Testament* (Grand Rapids: Zondervan, 1979).

Martin Luther, *Commentary on Galatians,* (Modern-English edition, Grand Rapids: Revell, 1998).

Alfred Marshall, *The Interlinear KJV-NIV Parallel New Testament In Greek and English* (Grand Rapids: Zondervan, 1975).

Iain H. Murray, *Spurgeon V. Hyper-Calvinism: The Battle for Gospel Preaching* (Edinburgh: Banner of Truth, 1995)

Hazel Offner, *Fruit of the Spirit: 9 studies for individuals and groups. LifeBuilder Bible Study Series* (Bletchley: Scripture Union, 1999).

Kenneth W. Osbeck, *Amazing Grace: 366 Inspiring Hymn Stories for Daily Devotions* (Grand Rapids: Kregel, 1990).

Clark H. Pinnock, *Truth On Fire: The Message of Galatians* (Grand Rapids: Baker, 1972).

John Piper, *A Godward Life: Book Two* (Sisters, OR: Multnomah, 1999).

John R.W. Stott, *The Message of Galatians* in The Bible Speaks Today series (Leicester: Inter-Varsity Press, 1988).

Thomas E. Trask, & Wayde I. Goodall, *The Fruit of the Spirit: Becoming the Person God Wants You to Be* (Grand Rapids: Zondervan, 2000).

W.E. Vine, Merrill F. Unger, William White Jr, *Vine's Complete Expository Dictionary of Old and New Testament Words* (Nashville: Nelson, 1984).